CALLED TO HELP THE
Poor & Needy

PATRICIA SAID ADAMS

Called to Help the Poor and Needy

Copyright © 2022 by Patricia Said Adams.

PB: ISBN: 978-1-63812-474-0
Ebook ISBN: 978-1-63812-475-7

All rights reserved. No part in this book may be produced and transmitted in any form or by any means, electronic, or mechanical, including photocopying, recording, or by any information storage and retrieval system, without permission in writing from the copyright owner.

The views expressed in this work are solely those of the author and do not necessarily reflect the views of the publisher hereby disclaims any responsibility for them.
Published by Pen Culture Solutions 10/21/2022

Pen Culture Solutions
1-888-727-7204 (USA)
1-800-950-458 (Australia)
support@penculturesolutions.com

Introduction..i

Chapter 1: *Biblical Teachings about the Poor and Needy*...............1

Chapter 2: *Who Is in Need?*..13

Chapter 3: *How Are We to Help the Poor and Needy?*.................21

Chapter 4: *Do We See Jesus in the Other?*....................................27

Chapter 5: *The Poor Will Always Be with Us*...............................33

Chapter 6: *Blessings and Curses*...39

Chapter 7: *Monarchs and the Wealthy*...45

Chapter 8: *Community*...51

Chapter 9: *Restorative Justice*...59

Chapter 10: *If We Take This Call to Help Seriously*.....................65

Chapter 11: *New Initiatives*..73

Chapter 12: *From Oblivion to Awareness*....................................81

Chapter 13: *Conclusion: Trust in God*...87

About the Author

Introduction

The notion for this book grew out of a call from God that I heard in January 2018 to do a video on helping the poor and needy. As I did the research for that video script, it became clear to me that this was a vast and complex subject that needed much more attention than a twenty-minute video. And so, I realized that I was being asked to write a book about this subject.

Until I looked at all the passages in the Bible about helping the poor and needy, I had no idea that it was a great theme of both the Old and New Testaments. There are more than two thousand verses about helping the poor, the needy, the stranger, and the foreigner. These are the people we judge them for not being worthy or not working hard enough. They don't look like us. They don't act like us. And so we separate ourselves from them. We see them as less than human. It is the stories we believe, that we tell about "those people," that determine how we treat them—and justify our treatment of them.

Consider the way many early white Americans "believed" the Africans brought to our country were less than human, so they could enslave them, beat them, separate them from their families, even lynch them—all because of the widespread belief among whites that Africans, and later African Americans, were not fully human beings. Slavery, and much of the early American economy, was built on this lie. The legacy of that belief system affects many of our fellow Americans today.

We can see this today as our president labels Latino immigrants "rapists" and "killers,"[1] as ICE pursues them, separating young children, even babies, from their parents. We provide subhuman quarters and no medical treatment to the detained. Our official American policy is that these immigrants are not worthy of being treated like human beings.[2]

And yet, these are the people who worry us, who remind us that we are vulnerable, too: might any of us be in their shoes someday?

> We forget that we, too, have been mistreated.
> We, too, have not lived up to others' expectations.
> We, too, have felt like strangers in some circles.
> We, too, have suffered slights and lack of essential things.
> We, too, have been injured.
> We, too, are not perfect human beings.
> We, too, share 99.99 percent of our DNA with every other human being.

We forget that God created this interdependent system of plants and animals and human beings. Every bit of creation and every creature, every human being is created by Him, and we need to honor it all, including all human beings, for the Creator ensures the survival of all species, be they plant or animal. There is not one person who is not a child of God, made in His image (Genesis 1:27). That is our legacy and our promise: that we are children of God and deserving of being treated as such, whether we are rich or poor, black or white, Latino or Asian, African or American. There are no differences

---

[1] Carolina Moreno, "9 Outrageous Things Donald Trump Has Said about Latinos," Huffington Post, August 31, 2015, updated November 9, 2016, https://www.huffpost.com/entry/9-outrageous-things-donald-trump-has-said-about-latinos_n_55e483a1e4b0c818f618904b.

[2] Dara Lind, "The Trump administration's separation of families at the border, explained," *Vox*, updated August 14, 2018, https://www.vox.com/2018/6/11/17443198/children-immigrant-families-separated-parents.

among us that can separate us from the love of God. All of us human beings are welcomed by God when we turn back to Him, when we repent and turn our lives around—no matter what we have done.

As a nation, we're conflicted about welfare. We have more people unable to afford medical care than any European nation, because of a fear that caring for those in need will earn us a label of socialism. In October 2019, the *New York Times* reported that there were a million fewer children covered by Medicaid in June of 2018 than in December of 2017.[3] How can we leave our children behind? How can we not care for them regardless of why they need coverage? This book's aim is to explore what the Bible says about taking care of the poor and needy, and then to ponder God's call to each of us about what we are to do for them.

Who should be helping the poor and needy? Is it just a job for the churches, as President George Bush proposed,[4] or should our public policy take on the full share of what our economy does to people on the margins? Do we think that all "welfare mothers" are scam artists, or do we see the great need in our country as our economy shunts aside the poor, the contract workers, as it closes the factories? As we pay the CEOs 940 percent more than they made in 1978 while the average worker's pay has gone up only 11.9 percent in that same period of time?[5]

Helping the poor and needy is not just about feeding and clothing and housing them. It's also about justice—the fair and equitable

---

3   Abby Goodnough and Margo Sanger-Katz, "Medicaid Covers a Million Fewer Children. Baby Elijah Was One of Them." *New York Times*, October 22, 2019, updated October 25, 2019, https://www.nytimes.com/2019/10/22/upshot/medicaid-uninsured-children.html.

4   "President George Bush announces plan for "faith-based initiatives," *History*, February 7, 2002, https://www.history.com/this-day-in-history/president-george-w-bush-announces-plan-for-faith-based-initiatives.

5   https://www.epi.org/publication/ceo-compensation-2018/

treatment of each and every person—and mercy: compassion for them, for their story, for the ways their lives have gone. God calls us to treat each and every person as someone of value who deserves our love and caring. That is what it means to follow Jesus.

The Lord has spent the last seventeen years preparing me for this subject. I have learned to embrace the people who have not enjoyed the privilege I have, through two trips to Haiti, a three-week stint at the Mexican-American Cultural Center in San Antonio, a month in Oaxaca watching life be truly celebrated by all at free outdoor events, a year interviewing clients at Crisis Assistance Ministry in Charlotte, and more. He has prepared my heart and soul to issue this invitation to Christians everywhere: to answer God's call to help the poor and needy.

I invite you to join me in looking at what God has said throughout the Old Testament, how Jesus continued the theme, and more. We'll study how the Israelites moved in and out of following God's laws. Most importantly, we will consider how to best see and hear what God is saying to each of us about our own attitudes and actions and how to see the Biblical commands in the light of God's love for all His people.

In writing this book, the conclusion that I have come away with is that we of higher income and socioeconomic status, especially we who are white, have a lot to learn about God and His ways from those whose more challenging economic circumstances have helped to create among them a community of connectedness and appreciation. This sense of community, of our interconnectedness, is a high value for the kingdom of God.[6] When we live in the kingdom of God, we welcome everyone regardless of education, income, race, or any differences that may be obvious on the surface. We celebrate what each person brings to the table and validate one another for what

---

6 In my book *The Kingdom Come!*, I compare the sense of community in the kingdom of God with the *agora,* the marketplace of ancient Greece.

is so obvious to anyone in the kingdom: we are all connected in the fiber of our being by the Spirit of the Living God who loves and forgives and binds us all together, because we were all made in God's image and are His children.

Come with me on this journey through the Old and New Testament. Read what God says about the poor and needy and how we are to help them. Most of all, connect to Jesus Christ through the Holy Spirit, and hear what He is saying to you about your own call to help the poor and needy. And then do what He asks.

Chapter 1:
Biblical Teachings about the Poor and Needy

Taking care of the poor and needy is a major theme in the Bible. It emerges in the Exodus story and continues through the Pentateuch (Leviticus, Numbers, and Deuteronomy), the historical books (Joshua through Esther), the poetic and wisdom writings (Job through the Song of Songs), the major prophets (Isaiah through Daniel), the minor prophets (Hosea through Habakkuk), and into the New Testament (especially in the four Gospels).

The Poverty and Justice Bible, published in 2009, highlights the more than two thousand verses that mention the poor and injustice in the Bible. Pastor Rick Warren, author of *The Purpose-Driven Life*, was an inspiration for this new version of the Bible. "It was US pastor Rick Warren who started the ball rolling. He has studied theology, he said, he'd been a pastor for decades—so how did he miss more than two thousand verses that speak of God's heart for the poor?"[7] We are called by God to help the poor and needy; if we do not, we are not in God's will.

The verses throughout this book represent the various shades of meaning the Bible gives to this call to serve the poor and needy and to deal with the injustices that cause economic and emotional and spiritual deprivation. The Ten Commandments do not specifically

---
7 https://biblesociety.ca/newsletters/Winter2009WaW/feature_1806.html

tell us to help others, but we are commanded not to murder, commit adultery, steal, lie, or covet anything that belongs to our neighbors. Any of those acts would impact our neighbor economically and emotionally. In relieving a neighbor of his property or his wherewithal; in violating his person, his wife, or children, envying or coveting what he has, a person will violate the last five commandments.

It is most of all a lack of gratitude to God for all that He has given us, including gratitude for our life here on this planet, that allows us to lie or cheat or covet or murder. When we look at what another has that we don't, or think how easy their life is compared to ours, when we let anger rule our lives, when we don't see our own sin and project it out onto another, when we don't accept our own pain and suffering—these attitudes of ours allow us to mistreat others, even to the point of murder.

Human beings were created in a certain way by God, our Creator. We were given certain freedoms, including free will. But the Ten Commandments reflect how we can best enjoy our lives and fulfill our creation: that is, by following these laws and the principles behind them, which Jesus reduced to two commandments: to love God with all of your heart, mind, soul, and strength, and to love your neighbor as yourself (Matthew 22:34–40, Mark 12:28–31, Luke 10:25–28). I believe these principles and laws also make up our consciences, so that when we follow our own innate, interior calibrator, we will actually be following God's laws. The same can be said for the first five commandments about God and our parents. If we again follow our consciences and put God first in our lives and honor our parents, we are again doing what we were created to do.

What makes our consciences and the commandments difficult to follow is that we each form a personal lens on life by age six. This lens is made up of a number of components: 1) the shame and/or guilt we felt at not being able to obey our parents' instructions; 2) what our families taught us about life; 3) any difficult or traumatic event in our lives; and 4) the values of the culture we grow up in. The more we are able to shed our own personal lens, which distorts what we see, the closer we come to following the innate principles of our creation, the more we are following God's laws, not the world's ways. And that is where we experience peace, joy, wonder, and gratitude—in expressing our truest selves.

The Pentateuch

With that background, let us turn to what God says in the first five books of the Bible about helping the poor and needy and fighting injustice. The strongest statement in the Pentateuch is this: "I command you to be openhanded toward your fellow Israelites who are poor and needy in your land" (Deuteronomy 15:11). God, while leading the Israelites through the wilderness, enumerates the attitude one should have:

> If the neighbor is poor, do not go to sleep with their pledge in your possession. Return their cloak by sunset so that your neighbor may sleep in it. (Deuteronomy 24:12–13)
> Pay them their wages each day before sunset, because they are poor and counting on it (Deuteronomy 24:14-15).
> If any of your countrymen become poor and are unable to support themselves among you, help them as you would a foreigner and stranger, so they can continue to live among you (Leviticus 25:35).
> If anyone is poor among your fellow Israelites in any of the towns of the land the Lord your God is giving you, do not be hardhearted or tight-fisted toward them (Deuteronomy 15:7).
> When you reap the harvest of your land, do not reap to the very edges of your field or gather the gleanings of your harvest. Do not go over your vineyard a second time or pick up the grapes that have fallen. Leave them for the poor and the foreigner. (Leviticus 19:9–10)
> Do not take a pair of millstones—not even the upper one—as security for a debt, because that would be taking a person's livelihood as security (Deuteronomy 24:6).

The principles God enumerates here boil down to: do not cheat or abuse or take a poor or needy person's essentials. And be generous.

A second theme beyond treating the poor well, not hurting them economically, and providing food for them is to do justice to them. Show mercy and compassion.

> Do not deny justice to your poor people in their lawsuits. Have nothing to do with a false charge and do not put an innocent or honest person to death. (Exodus 23:6-7)
> Do not pervert justice; do not show partiality to the poor or favoritism to the great, but judge your neighbor fairly (Leviticus 19:15).
> Do not show partiality in judging; hear both small and great alike. Do not be afraid of anyone, for judgment belongs to God. (Deuteronomy 1:17)

Isn't it interesting that God is not favoring the poor over the rich, but asking that the courts treat everyone fairly? This echoes Jesus's saying in Matthew 5 about how God created this world: "He causes his sun to rise on the evil and the good, and sends rain on the righteous and the unrighteous" (Matthew 5:45).

The Historical Books

In the historical books, Joshua through Esther, the Israelites began by overtaking most of the kingdoms of Canaan—thirty-one kingdoms in all, with God's help. When God distributed the land, it was equitably divided among the twelve tribes. And the tribes were to distribute the land equitably to their people as well. So, God gave them the land He had helped them conquer, a land he had promised to the descendants of Abraham, a land of milk and honey in which to prosper, to thrive.

Even before the division of land in Canaan among the tribes, God was expecting that the Israelites would not be able to hold to the law or to their worship of God (Deuteronomy 31:16). The pattern of the monarchy, of some rich and a lot of poor people, was the world's pattern and would prove tempting for the Israelites. It was during Samuel's reign that the elders came to Samuel and asked that he appoint a king to succeed him, because they didn't trust his sons. When Samuel told the Lord what his people asked, the Lord replied:

> "Listen to all that the people are saying to you; it is not you they have rejected, but they have rejected me as their king. As they have done from the day I brought them up out of Egypt until this day, forsaking me and serving other gods, so they are doing to you. Now listen to them, but warn them solemnly and let them know what the king who will reign over them will claim as his rights." (1 Samuel 8:7–9)

Samuel gave the warning as directed:

> "He will take your sons for his army or to plow his ground . . . your daughters for perfumers and cooks and bakers . . . the best of your fields and vineyards and olive groves . . . a tenth of your grain and vintage . . . your male and female servants and the best of your cattle and donkeys and flocks . . . you will become his slaves." (1 Samuel 8:11–17)

The Israelites did not listen to God, so they invited the kind of monarchy that had enslaved them in Egypt and that they had seen all throughout the wilderness and Canaan. So the Israelites were to suffer poverty and oppression.

The Poetic and Wisdom Writings

In the Psalms, the Lord hears the cries of His people as He did when they were slaves in Egypt.
> You evil doers frustrate the plans of the poor, but the Lord is their refuge (Psalm 14:6).

This poor man called, and the Lord heard him: he saved him out of all his troubles (Psalm 34:6).
The Lord hears the needy and does not despise his captive people (Psalm 69:33).
He raises the poor from the dust and lifts the needy from the ash heap (Psalm 113:7).
The Lord secures justice for the poor and upholds the cause of the needy (Psalm 140:12).
You [Lord] have been a refuge for the poor, a refuge for the needy in their distress, a shelter from the storm and a shade from the heat (Isaiah 25:4).

When Job has lost everything, including his health, God says that "His children must make amends to the poor, his own hands must give back his wealth" (Job 20:10), "for he has oppressed the poor and left them destitute; he has seized houses he did not build" (Job 20:19).

The story of Job is a cautionary tale for anyone who steals from or oppresses the poor. When Job stands humbled before God, He accepts this prayer:

Surely I spoke of things I did not understand, things too wonderful for me to know.
You said, "Listen now, and I will speak;
I will question you,
and you shall answer me."
My ears had heard of you
but now my eyes have seen you.
Therefore, I despise myself
and repent in dust and ashes. (Job 42:3-6)

God asked Job to pray for his friends and said that He would accept that prayer. Then "the Lord restored [Job's] fortunes and gave him twice as much as he had before" (Job 42:10). In a way, Job had to see himself as poor and needy, humbled before the Lord, before he was blessed.

The Major Prophets

By the time of Isaiah, around 700 BC, the monarchy was well established. And Isaiah cried out to the nation:

> Woe to the sinful nation,
> A people whose guilt is great,
> a brood of evildoers,
> children given to corruption!
> They have forsaken the Lord;
> they have spurned the Holy One of Israel
> and turned their backs on him. (Isaiah 1:4)

Isaiah is calling the people back to the sole worship of God and to following His laws, but not without warning them against deception and guiding them toward nobility.

> Scoundrels use wicked methods,
> they make up evil schemes
> to destroy the poor with lies,
> even when the plea of the needy is just.
> But the noble make noble plans,
> and by noble deeds they stand. (Isaiah 32:7–8)

The prophets, speaking for God, cry out for the poor and needy, and the Lord will answer their prayers. "I the Lord will answer [the poor]; I, the God of Israel, will not forsake them" (Isaiah 41:17). Jeremiah writes: "He defended the cause of the poor and needy, and so all went well. 'Is that not what it means to know me?' declares the Lord." (Jeremiah 22:16) There's a formula at work here: when we follow God's laws, we will be blessed; when we don't, we will be cursed.

Ezekiel, during the Babylonian exile, continued the condemnation of the Israelites in the sixth century BC.

> He eats at the mountain shrines.
> He defiles his neighbor's wife.
> He oppresses the poor and needy.
> He commits robbery.
> He does not return what he took in pledge.
> He does detestable things.
> He lends himself at interest and takes a profit. (Ezekiel 18:11–13)

God has warned His people all throughout the Old Testament that rampant disregard of His laws and failure to worship Him would cause great havoc in their nation.

The Minor Prophets

Amos, writing in the eighth century BC, again stressed following the law.

> Seek good, not evil,
> that you may live.
> Then the Lord God Almighty will be with you,
> just as you say he is.
> Hate evil, love good;
> maintain justice in the courts.
> Perhaps the Lord God Almighty will have mercy
> on the remnant of Joseph. (Amos 5:14–15)

But he wrote in chapter 8: "The Lord has sworn by himself, the Pride of Jacob: 'I will never forget anything they have done'" (Amos 8:7). We must not forget that our all-knowing God does know everything! All the prophets exclaimed about how far Israel had gone from the law and from God, but did the Israelites listen? No! Here is how Zechariah, writing in the late sixth century BC, reported their reaction:

> But they refused to pay attention; stubbornly they turned their backs and covered their ears. They made their hearts as hard as flint and would not listen to the law or to the words that the Lord Almighty had sent by his Spirit through the earlier prophets. So the Lord Almighty was very angry.
>
> "When I called, they did not listen; so when they called, I would not listen," says the Lord Almighty. "I scattered them with a whirlwind among all the nations, where they were strangers. The land they left behind them was so desolate that no one traveled through it. This is how they made the pleasant land desolate." (Zechariah 7:11–14)

The New Testament

Taking up the Old Testament theme of helping the poor and needy, Jesus quoted Isaiah at the beginning of His ministry in Nazareth:

> The Spirit of the Lord is on me,
> because the Lord has anointed me
> to proclaim good news to the poor.
> He has sent me to proclaim freedom for the prisoners
> and recovery of sight for the blind
> to set the oppressed free,
> to proclaim the year of the Lord's favor. (Luke 4:18–19)

Jesus is throwing down the gauntlet of God's care for the poor. In the Parable of the Sheep and the Goats, He goes even further when He says to the sheep: "Truly I tell you, whatever you did for one of the least of these brothers and sisters of mine, you did for me" (Matthew 25:40). When we help the poor and needy, we are caring for and serving the Lord Himself. The "goats" who did nothing to help the poor and needy are condemned to "eternal punishment" (Matthew 25:46).

In the book of Mark, Jesus tells two stories that pertain to our theme: one of the rich young man and the other of the poor widow. When the rich young man asks Jesus what he has to do to attain eternal life, Jesus replies, "Go sell everything you have and give to the poor, and you will have treasure in heaven. Then come, follow me." (Mark 10:21) The young man walks sadly away. And Jesus with great sympathy says to His disciples, "How hard it is for the rich to enter the kingdom of God" (Mark 10:23).

Later, in Mark 12, a poor widow drops two small coins into the offering—"all that she had to live on" (Mark 12:44). Jesus commented that she gave all of what she had while the rich gave out of their wealth. "Truly I tell you, this poor widow had put more into the treasury than all the others" (Mark 12:43).

Luke offers more about the poor and needy in five separate passages. In chapter 11, Jesus reams out the Pharisees who "clean the outside of the cup and dish, but inside you are full of greed and wickedness. You foolish people! Did not the one who made the outside make the inside also? But now as for what is inside you—be generous to the poor, and everything will be clean for you." (Luke 11:41)

He echoes this teaching in the next chapter when talking to the disciples about worry: "Do not be afraid, little flock, for your Father has been pleased to give you the kingdom. Sell your possessions and give to the poor. Provide purses for yourselves that will not wear out, a treasure in heaven that will never fail, where no thief comes near and no moth destroys. For where your treasure is, there your heart will be also." (Luke 12:32–4)

Jesus greatly extends this teaching when He dines at the home of a Pharisee. He tells the host and his guests not to invite their friends or relatives or rich neighbors to lunch or dinner, not to look to be repaid in this world, but to honor God's will and to treat the poor and needy without hope of compensation until "the resurrection of the righteous" (Luke 14:14).

He clearly emphasizes this lesson in the Parable of the Great Banquet, when none of the invited guests choose to come to the banquet. The master tells his servant, "Go out quickly into the streets and alleys of the town and bring in the poor, the crippled, the blind and the lame" (Luke 14:21). "Then the master told his servant, 'Go out to the roads and country lanes and compel them to come in so that my house will be full. I tell you, not one of these who were invited will get a taste of my banquet.'" (Luke 14:23–24)

Finally in Luke, there is Zacchaeus, a sinner, a tax collector, pledging to Jesus, "Look, Lord! Here and now I give half of my possessions to the poor, and if I have cheated anybody out of anything, I will pay back four times the amount." (Luke 19:8) All because Jesus sought him out and asked if He could stay at his house.

As we have walked through this tasting of God's care for the poor and needy throughout the Bible, it is clear that God has a heart for the poor and needy. He clearly wants us to take care of our neighbors, particularly those in need and foreigners. He wants us to treat them well in the courts. Jesus showed us how to hang out with the poor and oppressed. How to help them, to heal them. How to honor and value and feed them. How we are to see Jesus in everyone. How could we not acknowledge and follow these many instructions in His Bible? God is inviting us—no, commanding us—to be true to His desires for the poor and needy.

It is not enough to go to church every Sunday but fail to live up to the teachings during the rest of the week. Jesus asks for a total commitment of our lives. It is not enough to believe in Jesus as the

Son of God and in God the Creator of the Universe. It is only enough when we actually follow God's commandments and Jesus's teachings and base our actions and our voices in all that He taught us. And then, as we listen to the "still, small voice" of God who would lead every step that our lives take, we will be His disciples, His hands, and His love on this earth. And what a difference we would make in serving Him who lives in the other, in our neighbor, in the poor and needy.

Chapter 2: Who Is in Need?

When God talks about the poor and needy, who does He mean? The poor have some money, barely enough to get by; they may be incapacitated by illness or crippled and unable to support themselves. They may live on the edges of our society, unable to participate fully in education, in job opportunities and training, because they lack the resources. They live in inadequate housing, barely able to keep body and soul alive. They live in rural areas; they live in our cities and outside the suburbs. They live in trailer parks and on the streets. Everywhere they live on the margins, barely scraping together enough money to feed and house themselves, much less to thrive and get ahead.

In the Bible the Hebrew and Greek words for the poor and needy, most often *ani*[8] and *dal*[9] in Hebrew and *ptochos*[10] in Greek, are not just referring to a lack of money or resources, but also to an oppressed population and rejection by pretty much everyone. There is definitely a sense of systemic oppression in the words translated to "poor" in the Bible; the poor are not faulted for their personal bad choices.

In this country we tend to blame the poor for their condition: we say they should "pull themselves up by the bootstraps." They should get themselves educated so they can get a good job. But schools

---

8   "needy, poor, oppressed, often referring to people of low status and lacking resources": Goodrick & Kohlenberger III, *Zondervan NIV Exhaustive Concordance*, 2nd ed., (Grand Rapids, MI: Zondervan Publishing House, 1999), Strong's #6714, p. 1468.
9   "poor, needy, humble, weak, haggard, scrawny": Strong's #1924, p. 1389.
10 "poor, beggar, a person of few resources, culturally considered oppressed, despised, and miserable": Strong's #4777, p. 1588.

often do not adequately prepare them for upward mobility. They may have no expectations that any effort on their part would actually improve things. They may be stuck in low-end jobs with no hope for change. They may be living out the expectations of their families of origin. They may be emotionally scarred. They may be working so hard to make ends meet that they have little time or energy to explore other options. Unlike the post-World War II period when upward mobility was a viable option for returning white soldiers, with the G.I. Bill paying for college education and home loans, and with manufacturing jobs and unions assuring good pay, today there is little hope of upward mobility for the lower and middle classes. There are few manufacturing jobs; they've been outsourced to other countries with much lower pay standards than ours.

The huge difference between what a CEO makes and what one of his employees makes is even more startling when comparing today's numbers to those of the 1970s. In 1978 a CEO would earn thirty times the income of the typical American worker, or a 30:1 ratio. Now that ratio is 271:1. That's $15,000,000 for a CEO to $58,000 for an average worker. In real terms, the average CEO has seen a 937 percent increase in compensation since 1978; the average worker has received an 11.2 percent pay increase during the same period. According to business reporter Ruth Umoh, "CEOs are getting more because of their power to set pay, not because they are more productive or have special talent or more education."[11] Of course, higher pay for CEOs means that fewer dollars are available to the people actually doing the work.

Many people struggling under the weight of poverty have dreams that they have no time or resources to follow. Social entrepreneur Mauricio Miller was raised by a single mother who worked two jobs as sole support for her children. He remembers well his mother coming

---

11 Ruth Umoh, "CEOs make $15.6 million on average—here's how much their pay has increased compared to yours over the year," CNBC, January 22, 2018, www.cnbc.com/2018/01/22/heres-how-much-ceo-pay-has-increased-compared-to-yours-over-the-years.html.

home and exclaiming about a dress she had seen in a store window. She would talk about what she would do to improve it, but she had no time, money, or energy to pursue this love of dressmaking.

For most of my life, I had little contact with the poor. And I had no idea how they lived until I started interviewing them and hearing their stories. From 2013 to 2014, I worked as an interviewer for Crisis Assistance Ministry in Charlotte, North Carolina. The organization seeks to help community members through a financial crisis, often caused by a medical bill, a car breaking down, or anything outside their ordinary budget that proves impossible for them to pay.

The lowest rent in Charlotte at this time was $500 a month for a single person. Any crisis could easily eat up the month's rent. Some months, when FEMA money was available, the organization had up to $1,000 to give to clients in need. Without FEMA funds, we were limited to more like $150, an amount not sufficient to cover most crises. It was heart-wrenching to listen to people's stories and then total their financial assets and expenses, especially when we only had $150 to give. Usually, clients had no savings, no family members to back them up.

Here are some statistics on child poverty in the United States from 2015, courtesy of the Children's Defense Fund.

- In 2015 out of a population of 321 million Americans, 43.1 million fell within federal poverty guidelines; one in three were children. Nearly 20 percent of children in the US were considered poor in 2015.

- In 2015, poverty was defined as an annual income below $24,257 for an average family of four, meaning less than $2,021 a month, $466 a week, or $66.46 a day. More than 6.5 million children—one in eleven—lived in extreme poverty that year, with an annual income of less than half the poverty level, or $12,129 for a family of four.

- US children living in poverty (2015): 14,509,000

- US children living in extreme poverty (2015): 6,537,000

When we address an issue like poverty in our country or in the world, we must remember that we are commanded by God to take care of the poor and needy. Over and over in different words throughout the Old Testament God says,

> Defend the weak and the fatherless;
> uphold the cause of the poor and the oppressed.
> Rescue the weak and the needy;
> deliver them from the hand of the wicked. (Psalm 82:3–4)

In the New Testament, Jesus ups the ante, saying, "When you did it for the least of these brothers and sisters of mine, you did it for me" (Matthew 25:40). Every human being we encounter is also another face of Jesus in this world. We are to see the divine Christ in each human being. And doesn't that change everything? We can no longer hang onto our prejudices, our assumptions, our judgments, our critiques of others.

Hear Mother Teresa who took care of the sick and dying on the streets of Calcutta express this principle: "I see Jesus in every human being. I say to myself, this is hungry Jesus, I must feed him. This is sick Jesus. This one has leprosy or gangrene, I must wash him and tend to him. I serve because I love Jesus."

When we can see Jesus in every other person, we are seeing through the eyes of love, of compassion, of worship of the Lord, of forgiveness, of gratitude. And then the whole world is changed from our own personal, world-stained lens to God's view of every person He created, put a part of Himself in, endowed with certain gifts and talents, or launched with some challenges to overcome. Once we begin to see the person before us from the inside out, with an imprint of Jesus in him or her, we can never go back to our own personal view and judgment again.

It has been so interesting for me to read Father Gregory Boyle's two books, *Tattoos on the Heart* and *Barking at the Choir*. Since 1992, Father Boyle has worked with gang members in Central Los Angeles, recruiting a lot of them for jobs in Homeboy and Homegirl Industries. He walked the streets late at night to meet the gang members on their own turf. He got to know them, found out why they were in a gang and what their family life had been like. He tells story after story of their lives, often of the abuse they suffered, the absentee or abusive parents, the poverty and lack of opportunity, the hardships they have survived so far.

Through the softer, more loving approach of the Homeboy and Homegirl Industries, I have gotten a totally different image of these gang members. I have some understanding of why they've done what they've done and how they can change. I've had to give up my judgmental attitude toward gang members and acknowledge that given the right environment, they can become great workers and parents and citizens; they can go from being totally down on themselves (as they learned from their backgrounds) to being proud of who they are and what they do. They, too, are human beings made in the image of God.

From the Exodus story through the Psalms and the Prophets, God expressed His concern for the poor and needy. In Deuteronomy 15, when He is detailing the Ten Commandments, He commands the Israelites to take care of the poor: "There will always be poor people in the land. Therefore, I command you to be openhanded toward your fellow Israelites who are poor and needy in your land." (Deuteronomy 15:11)

In chapter after chapter, book after book of the Old Testament, God stresses His instructions for how we are to treat the poor. In Psalm 14:6, He says, "You evildoers frustrate the plans of the poor, but the Lord is their refuge." In Psalm 82:3–4, it's "Defend the weak and the fatherless; uphold the cause of the poor and the oppressed. Rescue the weak and the needy; deliver them from the hand of the wicked." And in the Psalms, there is lots of evidence of how God will rescue the weak: "The poor will eat and be satisfied" (Psalm 22:26). And "He raises the poor from the dust and lifts the needy from the ash heap; he seats them with princes, with the princes of his people. He settles the childless woman in her home as a happy mother of children." (Psalm 113:7–9) And more . . .

The Reverend Paul Hanneman, who was program director for fifteen years at the Urban Ministry Center in Charlotte, used to teach about the differences between the poor and the middle and upper classes. The highest value for the middle and upper classes in our country is education. Everything in their lives depends on how educated they are. For the poor, however, community is the highest value. We can see that high value placed on community in my son-in-law's trailer park in Florida, where the residents pitched in on rent when someone was short of cash. In how many middle- or upper-class neighborhood would neighbors talk to one another about money problems they were having?

Let us take the Biblical injunctions to take care of the poor and needy seriously and to heart. No longer are they to be "the other": the homeless or poor or sick. They are all—we are all–valued children of God, made in His image.

Chapter 3:

How Are We to Help the Poor and Needy?

How are we to help the poor and needy, and what are we to do for them or to give to them? The poor and needy are any persons, any human beings who need help, who are oppressed. In Matthew 25:35–36, Jesus defines our actions as giving food and drink, clothing, welcoming, and visiting the sick and imprisoned. I don't think He is limiting what we are to do, but rather being suggestive of the things we can do, maybe the most obvious things. He doesn't rule out all kinds of other help, not the least of which is being present to another person. He often asked the people He met, "What do you want?" (Matthew 20:32, Mark 10:51, Luke 18:41, among others). I am assuming He could see everything about the person before Him just like God sees, but still He asked what he or she wanted. He was present for the person and wanted to hear from them. He hung out with the poor and needy, the rejected, the disabled, the "unclean" like the Samaritan woman, and more. He was validating who they were and how important they were to Him by just being with them.

By extension, if we are to be present for any person before us, we have to get to know them, to hear what brought them to this point in their lives, their challenges and blessings, their sins, even, and what is good about them. For we were all made in the image of God. For every human being, there are two great needs, the need to love and be loved, and the longing to live in our true home, in God. Whether rich or poor, young or old, no matter our differences, we each need to be seen and to be loved. But of course, for the poor and needy, there is so much more we can do.

Hear how one of my blog readers who has been homeless three times tells it:

> We all have these social needs, the need to belong, or to love and be loved. Being loved is at its peak when we open up, share our true feelings, and find out that the other person accepts us and empathizes with us. This alone creates emotional intimacy between two people. When that need for love and that emotional intimacy are met, then people are happy and they become fulfilled. . . . The Homeless person just needs the assurance of another person and that there is someone who stands by his/her side to go through all these things, that everything will be okay. The importance that emotional intimacy can play in a person's life is what will give that person emotional support which will make him/her a whole person in the real sense of the word itself. The question is who is willing to step out of their comfort zone, and be a Good Samaritan, and give emotional support.[12]

When we bring God's love to our neighbors, no matter who they are or what they have been, we will see God's transforming work. Jesus commanded us to love our neighbors as we love ourselves. Do we even love ourselves? Aren't we another of God's children made in His image? Do we accept all that we have done and said, all that has been done to us? Or do we have to repress our pain or suffering, guilt and shame? Can we be people who can share all that we are, not just with God, but with our fellow human beings? Can we love ourselves, just as we are? Do we love our neighbors exactly as we love ourselves?

I believe that we cannot love another person if we cannot love ourselves, or forgive others for their sins if we cannot forgive ourselves

---

[12] David Samuel Davis, blog comment, *By the Waters*, May 16, 2017.

for what we have done and all that has been done to us. To love and forgive someone is to bring our whole selves to them. Just like the First Great Commandment of Jesus says to love God with all of ourselves, heart, soul, mind, and strength, that includes our sin and our good parts, our pain and our suffering, our gifts and our talents, our ego and all. Can we bring our whole selves to God? Or are we still hiding the "bad" parts, the guilt and shame? Can we bring our whole selves to our neighbors, too?

As we begin to love and forgive ourselves, we can begin to absorb God's love for us. And that changes everything. Then we don't just "know" about God's love for us in our minds; we feel God's love with all that we are. Loved and forgiven, we are totally new creations, much closer to who we were created to be by God. We may just have to start by accepting that God loves and forgives us and therefore we then can decide to love and forgive ourselves, too. It can be just an act of our will that gets us started. And then love can pour out of us into the people we meet, the words we say, the things we do.

Sometimes I think we stop short of what Jesus taught just so we don't have to change our lives. We concentrate on following God's commandments and forget about actually following Jesus. And there is a whole world of difference between the two. If we are just trying to obey the commandments, just trying to be good people, then we are like the Pharisees of Jesus's time: "You give a tenth of your spices—mint, dill, and cumin. But you have neglected the more important matters of the law—justice, mercy, and faithfulness. You should have practiced the latter, without neglecting the former." (Matthew 23:23) We want to look good on the outside, to others, but we neglect the motivations and hidden feelings that we have. And we are not really hearing what God and Jesus are saying about the law, and in this case, about helping the poor and needy.

If we are following Jesus, that means that we are led by Him, that we can hear His "still, small voice" (or "gentle whisper," in the NIV translation), that we are obeying what He suggests to us. We have set aside our own will and just live in His will. We are following His guidance in everything we say and do. That means He is the Lord of our marriage, of our work, of our leisure time, of our parenting, of everything that we are. He will show us what role we are to play with the poor and needy, just as He will for every other area of our lives: what we are to say and what we are to do. We no longer carry the burden of having to figure all this out. All we have to do is to be faithful to Him.

From the Exodus story through the Psalms and the Prophets, God expresses His concern for the poor and needy. In Deuteronomy 15, when He is detailing the Ten Commandments, He commands the Israelites to take care of the poor: "Give generously to them and do so without a grudging heart" (Deuteronomy 15:10).

In chapter after chapter, book after book in the Old Testament, God stresses His instructions for how we are to treat the poor. In Isaiah 10:1–2, He said, "Woe to those who make unjust laws, to those who issue oppressive decrees, to deprive the poor of their rights and withhold justice from the oppressed of my people." In Isaiah 1:17, it's "Learn to do right; seek justice. Defend the oppressed. Take up the cause of the fatherless; plead the case of the widow." And in the Psalms there is lots of evidence of how He will rescue the weak: "The poor will eat and be satisfied" (Psalm 22:26). And "He raises the poor from the dust and lifts the needy from the ash heap; he seats them with princes, with the princes of his people. He settles the childless woman in her home as a happy mother of children." (Psalm 113:7–9)

Isaiah says it best of all when he talks about fasting on behalf of other people:

> Is not this the kind of fasting I have chosen:
> to loose the chains of injustice
> and untie the cords of the yoke,
> to set the oppressed free

and break every yoke?
Is it not to share your food with the hungry
and to provide the poor wanderer with shelter—
when you see the naked, to clothe them,
and not to turn away from your own flesh and blood?
Then your light will break forth like the dawn,
and your healing will quickly appear;
then your righteousness will go before you,
and the glory of the Lord will be your rear guard.
Then you will call, and the Lord will answer;
you will cry for help, and he will say: Here am I. (Isaiah 58:6–9)

We usually think of fasting during Lent, giving up some food or other for the forty days, but Isaiah is talking about fasting for mercy and justice and caring for others, a giant step above what we usually entertain for Lent. He is talking about giving up what we enjoy so that others may have new life or liberty or food or help.

Our attitudes are clear in how we look at and think of the other person, the poor, the foreigner, the sick and lame, the prisoner, the slave. They are people created by God, too, and are deserving of our caring, too. In the courts, on the streets, in a restaurant, wherever. It's the maid in your hotel room, the servant, the waitress, the worker at Walmart, the gardener, the construction worker, the homeless. It's a person in grief or one who is gravely ill or has just lost his or her job. It's an ex-con. They are all human beings and deserving of our care, deserving of justice and mercy from all of us.

Get to know them, their stories, their hopes and dreams, and their traumas. Treat them well as you would one of your peers, one of your family, for we are all related through God. Value their existence and their contribution to the family of man. See the face of Jesus in each person. Show them love and mercy and compassion and justice. Do not compete with them or put them down or ignore them. For we are all in this life on this planet together. And we all suffer when any one of us suffers, even if we are not conscious of the suffering in us or in them.

If we take God's directives about the poor and needy, the stranger and the foreigner seriously, we will be pouring out God's love for them, we will be listening for the voice of the Lord, not what our church or preacher says, not what the congregation does, not what our friends do, and not what the culture says we should do. None of those are relevant when we hear the voice of the Lord speaking directly to us. And that voice will direct us toward justice, mercy, and love.

Chapter 4:
Do We See Jesus in the Other?

I think that we can look to Jesus's example when we consider the poor and needy in our lives and in our nation. Jesus spent time with the beggars, the outcasts, the sick, the lame, the tax collectors—all the rejected of His time. He healed them, He answered their prayers, He acknowledged their value, He embraced them, He fed them. He paid attention to the people who were lowest on the totem pole in His day. The ones who could not go into the temple because they were unclean. The ones who were prisoners of their conditions. The ones who had no standing in society.

What is He saying to us, today, in our technologically adept, post-industrial society? What is He saying to us about how we treat the poor and needy today? Let's listen to His words in Matthew 25:31–40. He talks about separating the sheep and the goats come judgment day. The sheep will go to the right, the goats to the left. He invites the sheep at his right hand to take up their inheritance in the kingdom of God: "Come, you who are blessed by my Father; take your inheritance, the kingdom prepared for you since the creation of the world. For I was hungry and you gave me something to eat, I was thirsty and you gave me something to drink, I was a stranger and you invited me in, I needed clothes and you clothed me, I was sick and you looked after me, I was in prison and you came to visit me."

The sheep represent those who treated people well, who see Jesus in every other person and treat each one accordingly. They not only take care of the physical needs of food and drink, but see to their spiritual needs: they visit them, sit down with them. They take care of the sick, welcome the stranger into their homes, visit the prisoner. There is no text more emphasized in all of the Gospels than this one. Jesus repeats his words to the sheep who asks when they had done all these things for Him. Jesus replies, "Whenever you did for one of the least of these brothers and sisters of mine, you did for me."

And He repeats it for the goats He is rejecting because they did not do all these things for him, saying, "Depart from me, you who are cursed, into the eternal fire prepared for the devil and his angels. For I was hungry and you gave me nothing to eat, I was thirsty and you gave me nothing to drink, I was a stranger and you did not invite me in, I needed clothes and you did not clothe me, I was sick and in prison and you did not look after me." And when the goats asked when they had done these awful things to Him, He replied, "Truly I tell you, whatever you did not do for one of the least of these, you did not do for me."

> Feed the hungry and thirsty.
> Clothe them.
> Welcome them into our lives.
> Visit and take care of the sick.
> Visit the prisoner.

So often we do one or maybe more off this list for the poor and needy, but we are also apt to give money for someone else to do it. Or if we do feed the poor or homeless, it's serving only their physical needs without getting to know them, entering into their life stories, meeting their spiritual and emotional needs. For with the poor and needy of any generation, the worst of the poverty is the isolation, the denigration of the poor. How are they to rise up out of their neediness if they don't feel wanted, valued, even, or affirmed for who they are, a child of God, made in His image? How are they to belong if no one ever treats them like they do?

Read more of what my blog reader wrote to me about his own homelessness.

> I used to hide my poverty, because it wasn't excepted [sic] in our society. Living in my car under the bridge, I kept all my clothes and personals there. I would wash up at a park's restroom and go into work, no one the wiser. I was living a double life . . . Life is hard and certain situations could put you in a bad spot, and then you have to begin to climb yourselves out of the hole. One of [the] things that people don't understand is the mental state that one goes through, going through so much. I've know[n] other veterans that experience the same outcome, because of lack of support system put in place. If we could only see beyond the visuals and imperfections, then we uncover discoveries that change all our lives.
>
> It's so inhumane how we can just brush across a homeless person, and not even think of them as people. But everyone has a story. No one is perfect. When I was on the street, it would take a special person to approach me. That person knew they would be opening a door, taking a chance. And I would be touch[ed] dearly for any chance or opportunity . . . It's the emotional connection that doesn't exist.[13]

We have to get to know the stranger, to know them well enough to value who they are and what they might contribute to the human community. It's not just the homeless, of course; it is every human being we encounter. We must see each one as a child of God, of infinite worth in His eyes, of being created in His image; we have to offer each one what we have been given. They need to know that God is on their side as well as ours. We must treat them as our neighbors who belong in our community. When Jesus said to love God with all of ourselves and our neighbors as ourselves, He meant that

---

13 David Samuel Davis, blog comment, *By the Waters*, April 26, 2018.

we are to embrace the neighbor, to value them, to affirm their existence, to love them, to treat them like they are Jesus Himself, for He resides in them just as He does in us. Our challenge is to see Jesus in every single person we meet, to see Jesus in ourselves. When we can see Jesus in ourselves, then it is much easier to see Jesus in every other person on this planet. In fact, it no longer takes any effort, because we can easily see in others what we now acknowledge in ourselves.

It's easy to use the word love, but what do I really mean? What do I think Jesus's definition of love would be? The definition I would choose is Paul's in Galatians 5:22–3: the fruit of the Spirit. To grow into the fruit of the Spirit means that we have long been walking the way with Jesus, learning from Him, being healed and transformed by His love. So that we are gifted with the fruit of the Spirit—peace, joy, love, patience, goodness, kindness, faithfulness, gentleness, and self-control. These definitions of love mean in total that we are trusting in the Lord to meet our needs so that we can fulfill the needs of others with true caring. Think of these fruits: being at peace; experiencing joy and love; having patience with ourselves and others; treating others with goodness, kindness, and gentleness; expressing our faithfulness to God; and exercising self-control. To exercise self-control as described here means to trust and to know that all our needs will be met, so that we can focus on the other person totally.

The core teaching that guides us is Jesus's directive to love our neighbor as ourselves, the second of the Two Great Commandments. The first is to love God with all of ourselves. When we can do this, the second part is easy. That's because we have already brought all of ourselves, sins and goodness, the human and divine within us, "the good, the bad and the ugly," as the old western movie title puts it, to God in love. When we can love ourselves enough to bring all of who we are to God in love, loving our neighbor is so easy.

When we love God with all of ourselves, we are laying on His altar the defensiveness, the anger, the rebellion, the fear we have endured for so long. We no longer need to wage any wars against the other, defend ourselves against any accusation, or rebel against God. We, who can love ourselves and love God, are at peace, finally and truly. We live without fear or anger. We are complete in who we are before God and our fellow men.

Here is how Father Richard Rohr puts it: "If you can't honor the Divine Indwelling—the presence of the Holy Spirit—within yourself, how could you see it in anybody else? You can't. Like knows like. All awareness, enlightenment, aliveness, and transformation begins with recognizing that your own eternal DNA is both divine and unearned; only then are you ready to see it everywhere else too. Soul recognizes soul."[14]

In order to love ourselves we may have to take to heart the Bible's assurances that we are loved, to undo the years of questioning, hating, fearing who we are, so that we can begin to love the person we have become and accept all that has happened to us. If we can begin to love ourselves, we may even be able to begin to take in God's love for us—just as we are. And as we take in His love, then the rigidities, the defensiveness, the pain and suffering begin to fall away, and we can truly stand before God just as we are.

And then we can pray Reverend Steve Garnaas-Holmes's prayer:

Crucified One,
give me grace to enter the wound of the world,
to accompany those who suffer,
to willingly suffer for others' sake,
not for the purpose that I meet you there,
which gives me joy,
but that I meet them there—
not that they may be a means to my joy,
but that I be a means to theirs.
Help me trust that you are with me on the cross

---

14 Father Richard Rohr, Daily Meditation, email of April 9, 2018.

not for my sake but for theirs.
Let your love in me overwhelm my fear
and transform my selfishness.
Give me true self-giving love,
which is the only joy.
Amen.[15]

---

15 Rev. Steve Garnass-Holmes, unfoldinglight.net, email of February 19, 2018.

Chapter 5:
The Poor Will Always Be with Us

Twice in the Bible we find the statement that there will always be poor people, once in Deuteronomy and once in the Gospel of Matthew. In Deuteronomy 15:11, God says that "there will always be poor people in the land. Therefore, I command you to be openhanded toward your fellow Israelites who are poor and needy in your land." This quote is one of many in the Old Testament in which God insists that all the people take care of those who are needy. We find God's admonitions to help and defend the poor in many places:

> "Do not deny justice to your poor people" (Exodus 23:6).
> "If any of your countrymen becomes poor . . . help them as you would a foreigner or a stranger" (Leviticus 25:35).
> "Give generously to them and do so without a grudging heart" (Deuteronomy 15:10).
> "Do not oppress the widow or the fatherless, the foreigner or the poor. Do not plot evil against each other." (Zechariah 7:10)

When we come to Jesus at the end of His life, He repeats the sentiment: "The poor you will always have with you," and then adds, "but you will not always have me" (Matthew 26:11). He is defending the actions of the woman who poured an alabaster jar of perfume on his head to his disciples, who were aghast at the expense and waste. But Jesus is making another point entirely: This is the end of His life, and she is preparing His body for burial, since He will soon be crucified. In a way He is saying, "Stay with me now, take care of me, for I will die this week. When I am gone, you can take care of the poor as always."

Unfortunately, many Christians have taken this to mean that since we'll always have the poor, we don't really need to bother ourselves a whole lot with them. Jesus is much more important to us. In interpreting His saying in this way, we ignore a major theme in the entire Bible, both in the Old Testament and the New. We ignore God's laws, His admonitions, His commands, His ways—all that He has told us to do.

The prophet Isaiah in chapter 58 puts the right emphasis on this whole issue of the poor when he speaks of the kind of fasting, the abstaining, that he chose to help the poor, as referred to in the last chapter. He continues detailing the benefits of that help:

> If you do away with the yoke of oppression,
> with the pointing finger and malicious talk,
> and if you spend yourselves in behalf of the hungry
> and satisfy the needs of the oppressed,
> then your light will rise in the darkness,
> and your night will become like the noonday.
> The Lord will guide you always;
> he will satisfy your needs in a sun-scorched land
> and will strengthen your frame.
> You will be like a well-watered garden,
> like a spring whose waters never fail. (Isaiah 58:9–11)

His use of the word fasting suggests many nuances in my mind. Fasting is denial of self, like a Lenten fast. It is a choice we make to devote ourselves to something while we give up something for ourselves. During Lent we might choose not to eat certain things, or only eat at dinnertime as a friend of mine does for those forty days. But Isaiah is speaking of self-denial in order to help the poor and needy, of choosing to deny time or money or some food to ourselves that others might live.¹⁶ He would have us fight injustice and set the oppressed free. He would have us work to change how society is doing things. He would have us work for the rights of the poor. We would share our food, shelter, and clothing. We would fast in order to be obedient to God's word.

Isaiah speaks of the benefits of spending ourselves on behalf of the poor and oppressed in Isaiah 58. "Your light will rise in the darkness," "The Lord will guide you always." Your needs will be taken care of; He will strengthen you. "You will be like a well-watered garden, like a spring whose waters never fail" (Isaiah 58:10–11). Jesus is echoing Isaiah in the Beatitudes when He says, "Blessed are the merciful, for they shall be shown mercy" (Matthew 5:7). To be merciful means to be compassionate, forgiving, humane, kind, generous, and more.

And didn't Jesus show this mercy everywhere He went? When he met lepers and the lame and blind and outcasts (Mark 1:31)? When He fed the crowd of five thousand (Matthew 14:13–21? When He challenged the Pharisees about following the law (Mark 7:1–9)? When He spoke with the Samaritan woman (John 4:1–26) and the Roman Centurion (Matthew 8:5–13) and others who were ritually unclean? Are we who follow Jesus doing what He did for the poor and needy? Do we deny ourselves that others might eat or have clothes to wear or be valued by us or listened to or helped out of oppression? Do we forgo some pleasures in order that others might thrive?

Do we see Jesus in the person who needs help? Do we associate the other with Jesus? Does He live in every other person? Do we take care of Jesus by serving another? The Parable of the Sheep and the Goats makes this point with great emphasis (Matthew 25:31–46). The questions for each of us are: Do I see the face of Jesus in every

---

16 Just writing about this passage, about fasting in this way, has changed how I eat and what I will offer to God as a fast on behalf of the poor.

human being, or do I pick and choose who I want to help? Am I willing to fast in the tradition of Isaiah, so that others might live?

We who are followers of Jesus, not just believers in Him, will do this kind of fast. We will work for the rights of the poor and needy. We will feed and clothe and visit and house them. We will listen to God's call for us in how and when and whom we are to serve, but it is clear that we serve Jesus in serving others. It is clear that we are to follow His example. That we are to do this kind of fast.

I think that God and Jesus point to something way beyond just doing physical things for the needy; certainly, Jesus carried on a dialogue with the people he met. When He asked people, "What do you want?", He then healed them of their problems, from crippling conditions to exorcising demons to excess blood flow. He was interested in them, invested in them; He asked them to follow Him. This points us beyond just "helping the poor" to actually entering into their lives, to find out how they came to be the person they are. To hear their stories and affirm their value. To love them as they are. To offer them a relationship with God through Jesus Christ, not because they've done some wrong, but because they, too, are made in the image of God.

To do this kind of fasting, we would have to give up our repugnance, our judgments, our labeling of the other, and choose to enter into his or her life's story in order to show them love. There is a huge difference between the poor and the rich in this country and elsewhere. The rich live separate lives. They need little from each other except for acknowledgement of their status above all the rest. They are always striving for more and more—approval, money, status; they are truly of this world.

And the poor? They will always be with us and, therefore, we are to take care of them. The Old Testament and Jesus's words and actions say the same thing: We must extend ourselves to see that the poor are taken care of. And do not in any way oppress them, cheat them, steal from them what is theirs. This kind of fasting is contrary to the ways of men and women who are always seeking to better themselves by hurting or using others—from slavery to outright thievery. These are not God's ways. He made the system to work equally well for all people; "He causes his sun to rise on the evil and the good, and sends rain on the righteous and the unrighteous" (Matthew 5:45). When He distributed land in Canaan to the Israelites, He did it equitably (Joshua chapters 13–21). If we are followers of Jesus, if we love God, we must follow His Word and take care of one another.

Chapter 6:
Blessings and Curses

After bringing the Israelites out of slavery in Egypt, and during years of wandering in the desert, God spends quite a bit of Leviticus, Numbers, and Deuteronomy detailing the Ten Commandments so that they apply to how we treat our neighbor, whether they are Israelites or strangers, how we deal with our neighbors' animals, our own servants and family members, how we are to worship the Lord, our God, and more. He also goes into great detail about who will make and care for all the things of worship. He assigns purposes to various tribes and individuals. Toward the end of Deuteronomy, the Lord sets out the principles of the law and the reasons for following it.

In chapter 28, He details the blessings that will come if we follow the law (verses 1–14) and all its implications—and the curses that will fall to us if we don't (verses 15–68). These consequences and the law express the process for success or failure for us as human beings. God is not waiting to punish us but pointing out that our punishment or blessing arises from the choices we make. If we choose to follow his law, we will experience blessings; if not, we will be cursed—either is the outcome we have chosen. Setting aside the world's terms of monetary and social success, He has shown us the way to lead fulfilled lives in the community of all the peoples of this Earth. If we love our neighbors and treat others as we like to be honored and valued and welcomed, we will prosper. I do not think that God is promising us wealth, rather that all we do and are will be affirmed. We won't have to worry about the paranoia and fear and defensiveness—the burdens, the yoke—that monetary wealth normally brings.

I believe that what He said in Deuteronomy 28 expresses another truth about us: that we are designed to thrive when we follow God's laws and to not thrive when we don't. It's all in our DNA, and it's echoed in our conscience.

How we treat each other determines the basics of our existence: Will we live in joy and love and peace or in despair and anger and defensiveness? It is clear in this chapter of Deuteronomy that we choose our own fate, that it is our choices that produce blessings and curses. If we follow His commands, we will be blessed.

You will be blessed in the city and blessed in the country.

> The fruit of your womb will be blessed, and the crops of your land and the young of your livestock . . .

> Your basket and kneading trough will be blessed.

> You will be blessed when you come in and blessed when you go out.

> The Lord will grant that the enemies who rise up against you will be defeated before you. They will come at you in one direction but flee from you in seven.

> The Lord will send a blessing on your barns and on everything you put your hand to. The Lord your God will bless you in the land he is giving you.

> The Lord will establish you as his holy people, as he promised you on oath, if you keep the commands of the Lord your God and walk in obedience to him." (Deuteronomy 28:3–9).

Next, He details what will happen if we disobey His commandments.

You will be cursed in the city and cursed in the country.

Your basket and your kneading trough will be cursed.

The fruit of your womb will be cursed, and the crops of your land, and the calves of your herds and the lambs of your flocks.

You will be cursed when you come in and cursed when you go out.

The Lord will send on you curses, confusion, and rebuke in everything you put your hand to, until you are destroyed and come to sudden ruin because of the evil you have done in forsaking him. (Deuteronomy 28:16–20)

If someone offends God by mistreating the poor and needy, there are consequences. If you don't pay their wages daily, "You will be guilty of sin" (Deuteronomy 24:15). In regard for how the Israelites were to treat their male and female slaves, "You must not rule over your fellow Israelites ruthlessly" (Leviticus 25:46). When the jubilee year rolls around every seven years, "Do not send [your former slaves] away empty-handed. Supply them liberally from your flock, your threshing floor and your winepress. Give to them as the Lord has blessed you." (Deuteronomy 15:13–14)

We choose to be blessed or cursed. What happens to us is the logical outcome of our following God's laws or not. If we follow His laws, then we will be blessed in all that we do. If we opt to disobey His laws, then we will live in paranoia and fear, trying to dodge any punishment for our sins.

We choose the consequences of our actions as we choose what we do and say. We choose to live in harmony with other people or to always put ourselves first. We choose to live in blessings and grace or in defensiveness and hostility. We choose to follow God's commands or to disobey Him. We choose our own future welfare or disaster. This doesn't mean we will never suffer if we choose to follow God. Or that we will be rich if we do. But if we listen to our own consciences telling us what to do and not to do, with us knowing the ramifications of our actions, and still choosing to disobey God, we might as well prepare for the worst.

God doesn't have to punish us; we've elected to be punished, if we disobey Him. He doesn't have to raise a hand to us; we did it to ourselves. We often blame God for any punishment or suffering we endure, but it is not on His shoulders. If we are defensive, angry, hostile even, it behooves us to look back on the decisions we have made to see when and how we went astray from God's ways and teachings. Think of our own humanity, our own sinfulness, and how Jesus handled the sinfulness of the Pharisees who brought a woman who had committed adultery to test Jesus. His reply: "Let any one of you who is without sin be the first to throw a stone at her" (John 8:2–11). And the crowd melted away. Not one could accuse her. Jesus then asked her to go and sin no more.

I am not in any way suggesting that any painful circumstance we endure is the result of our disobeying God. In other writings, I have suggested that our tenure here on earth is a school in which we are to achieve our created purpose, if we embrace the lessons that are offered to us. Just as in this case—we can learn from the times we turned away from God's ways. Or we can refuse to learn. But pain and suffering do not always result from our sin; they may just be the next lesson we need to learn on our journey toward living out our full, created purpose.

This doesn't mean that we won't get rich through our disobedience; that could be our fate, but we will never be able to enjoy it. We will have to build up walls to protect ourselves from these awful consequences; we will be on the lookout always for the worst to befall us. We will never be able to relax, to savor anything. The toll it will take on us to mistreat our fellow man so that we may prosper—we just have to expect the curses to fall on us. The more we go down the path of curses, the unhappier and more paranoid we will be. Jesus makes it clear that those who don't help their fellow man "will go away to eternal punishment, but the righteous to eternal life" (Matthew 25:46).

This is the system we live in. Having created us and knowing us so well, God makes it clear how we are to live, how we are to worship Him, how we are to be with our neighbors and strangers, how we are to thrive. It is our choice what befalls us. There is always the chance to turn back to God and to His ways. Repentance can change the whole course of our lives.

God favors neither the rich nor the poor; He created the world and this whole interdependent system that we live in for the benefit of all. And so are we to act on behalf of the poor, including them in the bounty of the land. He does not condemn the rich, but He does expect all of us to take care of the poor, to share out of our own blessings, just as God provided for the Israelites in Canaan (Deuteronomy 15:4). Neither the rich nor the poor are condemned or idealized. They all are simply some of now seven billion people who live on this earth. But those of us with resources to spare are to expend them on the poor, so that they will not suffer needlessly.

We are to have a heart for the poor, but not to condemn any man, for don't they do as we do, more or less? Don't we all run afoul of God's Law? Think of the way Jesus looked on the rich young man who couldn't give up his wealth—with love and compassion, too; rather than chide him, Jesus empathized with how hard it is for the rich to go through the narrow gate of the kingdom of God (Matthew 19:24).

The way we treat any man or woman counts. If we are good, kind, and gentle along with the rest of the fruit of the Spirit, then we are treating others as God has taught us, as God created us to be and to act. If we are defensive, judging, and hostile toward anyone, we are rejecting this person's humanity and not caring for him or her. And in fact, as egocentric as we are, we mostly struggle to love ourselves, much less another person.

God's covenant is with the whole tribe of Israel, not just with any individual. It's about community, always: our church community, our neighbors, our family and friends, all of God's people. His law gives high priority to community in how we treat each other. This is how God made us: to thrive in our lives or to demean them. That is why there are blessings when we treat people well and curses when we don't. The blessings reflect the actions that enhance our lives and the lives of our communities; the curses reflect our failure to care for others. It is all about community.

The context for our behavior in this world as set by God in Deuteronomy 28 is this: Our choices have consequences, which should be assessed as we decide to do anything. If we follow His law and the spirit of the law, we will be blessed. If we choose to violate His law and the spirit of the law, then we will be cursed. It's not that God is waiting to punish us for our actions; the consequences are built into any choice we make.

Chapter 7:
Monarchs and the Wealthy

Even as God at the end of Deuteronomy was preparing Moses for his death and the Israelites to enter Canaan, He was predicting that they would not be able to hold to the Law in the future. "These people will soon prostitute themselves to the foreign gods of the land they are entering. They will forsake me and break the covenant I made with them." (Deuteronomy 31:16) And later, even as the elders asked Samuel to appoint a king to succeed him, because not one of his sons was following his ways, God knew what had happened in the Israelite community. God told Samuel to warn the people that a monarch would confiscate all that they owned plus their sons and daughters would have to serve the king. He would take their servants and the best of their animals and crops. But the people did not listen. (1 Samuel 8:7–11)

In essence, the Israelites rejected God's sovereignty over them in favor of a human king. Kingdoms were the pattern of governance in the Middle East in these times, from the Pharaoh in Egypt to the kings of Canaan. The elders had asked Samuel for a king because they didn't trust Samuel's sons, who were corrupt. But the pattern of the monarchy soon became clear in the kings following Samuel.

In his book *There Shall Be No Poor Among You: Poverty in the Bible*, Old Testament scholar Leslie J. Hoppe, OFM, details the curses that the monarchy brought to the people of God. It "abetted the concentration of wealth in the hands of a privileged elite and the reduction of many—especially subsistence farmers—to poverty."[17] The king would "appropriate people and property through forced labor and heavy taxation, all to support his lavish lifestyle."[18] If the poor couldn't pay their taxes, then he confiscated their land and "made life very difficult for the Israelite peasant farmer . . . [forced] them into hired workers at best and beggars at worst. The monarchy . . . created poverty in Israel."[19]

It wasn't just the monarch that reaped the benefits of his reign, but his advisors and friends became rich, too. Soon after the even distribution of the land that God had overseen in Canaan for the Israelites, even before the kings ruled Israel, greedy hands began to use some of these methods to gain more land and ended up enslaving the poor, from being in debt to the wealthy and ultimately losing their land to being slave labor in the land that God had given them. Of course, throughout the Middle East at this time, this was the pattern. The Israelites were merely adopting the methods that had been used on them in Egypt and that they had seen in Canaan.

In the prophets, we find the details of their powerful assault on the poor and needy. Isaiah speaks of "unjust laws," "oppressive decrees to deprive the poor of their rights and withhold justice from the oppressed of my people, making widows their prey and robbing the fatherless" (Isaiah 10:1–2).

According to the prophet Ezekiel, "The people of the land practice extortion and commit robbery; they oppress the poor and needy and mistreat the foreigner, denying them justice" (Ezekiel 22:29).

Zechariah reminded the Israelites what the Lord had told them: "Administer true justice, show mercy and compassion to one

---

17 Leslie J. Hoppe, OFM, *There Shall Be No Poor Among You: Poverty in the Bible*, Abington Press (Nashville, TN: 2004) 54.
18 Hoppe, 55.
19 Hoppe, 55.

another. Do not oppress the widow or the fatherless, the foreigner or the poor. Do not plot evil against each other." And did they listen to the prophet? No! "They refused to pay attention; stubbornly they turned their backs and covered their ears. They made their hearts as hard as flint and would not listen to the law or to the words that the Lord Almighty had sent by his Spirit through the earlier prophets." (Zechariah 7:8–12)

It is interesting that God neither idealizes the poor nor condemns the rich. He simply expects the rich to help the poor. He simply expects all the Israelites to take care of their countrymen, "help them as you would a foreigner or a stranger, so that they may continue to live among you" (Leviticus 25:35). "Do not pervert justice, do not show partiality to the poor or favoritism to the great, but judge your neighbor fairly" (Leviticus 19:15).

As for later political systems ruling Jerusalem and the Israelites, the Persians ruled Jerusalem for two hundred years after the Babylonian exile around 720 BC. As usual, they extracted wealth to send it home to Persia. The same with the Romans. The tax collectors Jesus met took money from the people to send back to Rome and kept a portion for themselves. When Zacchaeus, a chief tax collector, met Jesus, he repented and swore that he would pay back four-fold what he had taken from the people (Luke 19:1–10).

The Bible does not rail against the wealthy for their wealth, only for the ways that they obtained it, if they seized it from the poor. Today we see the same methods used by the corrupt wealthy to take from the poor. A recent *New York Times* article pointed to the problems with rent control in New York City: "Affordable housing is vanishing as landlords exploit a broken system, pushing out rent-regulated tenants and catapulting apartments into the free market."[20] This is just one example of how the rich can exploit the poor. The

---

20 Kim Barker, "Behind New York's Housing Crisis: Weakened Laws and Fragmented Regulation," *New York Times*, May 20, 2018.

same techniques have been used by the wealthy for thousands of years.

The problem is not with the wealth, but with the abuse and oppression of the poor. Dr. Walter Brueggerman, an Old Testament scholar now retired, spoke in Charlotte in the spring of 2018 of our context, an unjust economy. He concluded that:

1. We have come to accept as normal an extraction economy, which uses up resources and capital without renewing them.[21]
2. The Bible proposes an alternative: an economy built on generosity and justice, a neighborly one.
3. There is a real tension between the extractive and neighborly economies. It is not the work of the church to ease this tension, but to face it.
4. As we face this tension, we must be aware of two kinds of people who contribute nothing to our economy: those have- and do-nothings who sit all day, and the nonproducers at the top of the economy systems in which powerful people extract their wealth from vulnerable people.[22]
5. In the Christian tradition, the Eucharist has come to be about sin, but it is really about gratitude for the manna God provided. Gratitude leads to generosity. Without gratitude, there is only greed. In God's world there is enough for everyone, but the American economy does not take care of its marginalized people.[23]

---

21 Stephen Hinton, "What is the extractive economy?", Medium.com, May 20, 2018, https://medium.com/@stephenjhinton/explainer-what-is-the-extractive-economy-65172f28bd6.

22 Ken Camp, "Old Testament offers relevant critique of economic injustice, Brueggermann says," Baptiststandard.com, November 9, 2016, https://www.baptiststandard.com/news/texas/old-testament-offers-relevant-critique-of-economic-injustice-brueggemann-says/.

23 My notes from Walter Brueggerman, speech at First Presbyterian Church, Charlotte, NC, March 4, 2018.

If our economy is an extraction economy, just like the economy of the monarchies of ancient Israel, how do we reconcile our democratic values with the desire of the rich to get richer and their indifference toward the poor and what happens to them? Since our economy favors the rich, they can denigrate the poor, take all that they can manage from them, refuse to support any legislation that would grant them release from the debt incurred because of laws that favor the rich. Top executives can boost their own pay tremendously and pay few increases to workers.

Such disparities are not limited to the workforce. In the *Charlotte Observer* on June 7, 2018, a report on public school districts in North Carolina revealed a systemic problem of keeping low-income children with superior test grades out of advanced math classes. The problems persist; even children are denigrated.

Should we allow schools to discriminate against low-income students? Should we let cities and counties add court charges for people they know can't afford them and so they land in jail for nonpayment? Should we let wealthy CEOs and other top executives to get rich on the backs of their employees, who are paid a small fraction of the CEOs' salary and benefits? Should we allow tax breaks for the wealthy without similar breaks for the poor? Where do we draw the line? Where are God's rules about taking care of everyone equally? What happened to upward mobility in our country, or was that only ever for the already wealthy?

What of the Emma Lazarus poem engraved on the Statue of Liberty?

Give me your tired, your poor,
your huddled masses yearning to breathe free,
the wretched refuse of your teeming shore.
Send these, the homeless, tempest-tossed to me,
I lift my lamp beside the golden door!

This was the promise of the New World that would relieve the poor and needy of the oppression of the Old World. And here we are today heading toward an economy like the Middle Ages with two classes of people, the rich and the very poor. We resemble little of what America was like after World War II, that time of great productivity when all economic classes had hope for upward mobility. Now that is gone.

Chapter 8:

Community

God's covenant is with the whole Israelite community, not with any individual. It was not about Moses and God or Joshua and God. By extension it is never about just me and God, or any other one person and God or the Israelites and God; it is about God Himself and all the people He created. After all, we were all made in "in our image, our likeness" (Genesis 1:26), a reference to a plural concept of God. God, as later revealed, is God the Father, Jesus Christ, and the Holy Spirit. The first community. And our model.

God's covenant with His people is about their relationship with Him, about including more than just God Himself. In our case, it's about more than each one of us; it's about the community. God is about the Trinity and all creation. And if we are to model ourselves after Christ and God and the Holy Spirit, we are together with all people: the rich and the poor, the young and the old, the oppressed and the free—every single person alive today that God cares about. And so should we, if we are to serve God. After all, DNA studies show that there is less than 0.1 percent difference among all human beings, regardless of race, ethnicity or any other differences that we may think are important. [24]

---

24 "One Species, Living Worldwide," Smithsonian National Museum of Natural History, humanorigins.si.edu/evidence/genetics/one-species-living-worldwide.

As Father Richard Rohr writes: "Community seems to be God's strategy and God's leaven inside the dough of creation. It is both the medium and the message. It is both the beginning and the goal: 'May they all be one . . . so the world may believe it was you who sent me . . . that they may be one as we are one, with me in them and you in me.'"[25]

In his book *The Inner Experience*, twentiety-century Trappist monk Thomas Merton wrote about his depth of experience in the Christian life:

> There is no other form for the Christian life except a common one. Until and unless Christ is experienced as a living relationship between people, the Gospel remains largely an abstraction. Until Christ is passed on personally through faithfulness and forgiveness, through the concrete bonds of union, I doubt whether he is passed on by words, sermons, institutions, or ideas.[26]

Jesus modeled this beautifully: he talked to the rich and powerful, the Pharisees and scribes, the poor and the marginalized. He served the crowds both teachings and food. He asked to be invited into a tax collector's home (Luke 19:5). He met with Pharisees and answered their complaints (Luke 5:30–31). He challenged them to include people not like them:

> When you give a luncheon or dinner, do not invite your friends, your brothers or sisters, your relatives, or your rich neighbors. If you do, they may invite you back and so you will be repaid. But when you give a banquet, invite the poor, the crippled, the lame, the blind, and you will be

---

25 Father Richard Rohr, "Reality in Communion," daily email, Sunday, May 6, 2018.
26 Thomas Merton, *The Inner Experience: Notes on Contemplation*, (San Francisco: Harper, 2003), 22.

blessed. Although they cannot repay you, you will be repaid at the resurrection of the righteous. (Luke 14:12–14)

Above all, He told parables that challenged the norms of the day, stories that made people stop and think. If Jesus taught us one thing, that is to be at home with every person you meet, because they all belong to God, even if they don't yet know it. His very words invite and challenge us today to include everyone.

Archbishop Desmond Tutu writes in his book *God is not a Christian and Other Provocations* about the African concept of *ubuntu*:

> [*Ubuntu* is] the essence of being human. It speaks of how my humanity is caught up and bound inextricably with yours. It says, not as Descartes did, "I think, therefore I am" but rather, "I am because I belong." I need other human beings in order to be human. The completely self-sufficient human being is subhuman. I can be me only if you are fully you. I am because we are, for we are made for togetherness, for family. We are made for complementarity. We are created for a delicate network of relationships, of interdependence with our fellow human beings, with the rest of creation.[27]

Rob Bell, author, speaker and former pastor, would go even further in describing the interrelationships that are always present among human beings:

> So when Jesus calls us to love our neighbor, there is more than just a command or an ethical statement or a rule of life. It's a truth about the very nature of reality. We are deeply connected with everybody around us, and our inten-

---

27 Desmond Tutu, *God Is Not a Christian and Other Provocations* (New York: HarperOne, 2011), 21–22.

tions and words and thoughts and inclinations toward them matter more than we can begin to comprehend.[28]

We all are already deeply connected, whether we are aware of any connections at all. Bell continues:

That's God all in all, bringing together all of our bodies and our minds and our souls and our spirits and all the parts and pieces that make us *us*, as our eyes are opened

> In
> the good,
> the bad,
> the ugly,
> the beautiful,
> the inspiring, and the
> gut-wrenching
> to the presence in all of life of the God who is with us,
> for us,
> and ahead of us.[29]

We are already deeply connected to every other human being through our Creator and through the interdependent system He created. That is the reality whether or not we are aware of it. When we can bring this truth to the conscious mind, then we can begin to behave in ways that reflect our interconnectedness and interdependence.

We can think of many communities to which we each belong. I have a GALS (Gratitude, Affirmation, Love, Spirit) group that meets twice a month to share, to study, to be real, and to grow. I belong to a band of the Wesleyan Contemplative Order that meets once a month to do centering prayer. A Presbyterian church is my primary

---

28 Rob Bell, *What We Talk About When We Talk About God* (New York: HarperOne, 2013) 202.
29 Bell, 207.

spiritual home. I have several circles of friends: old, dear friends in California; new friends in Charlotte, also dear. I have my whole family of origin and my husband's family, too. There are my three children, their spouses, and their children. I am a spiritual director and belong to a loosely tied community of spiritual directors. I am a part of my neighborhood. My city. The state of North Carolina. The United States of America. And the whole people of the world. That's a lot of communities!

God didn't just create a man, but also a woman to be his companion, both in His image. And they had children. And their children had children. And so on. God's intention was not that we live some isolated existence without others to help and support and guide and love us. When we replicate God's plan for us in our lives, we live in a deeply connected way to other people. That is the plan: the interconnectedness of us all through our creation by God and the ties that the Indwelling Holy Spirit promotes among us.

When we think of the Bible as suggestive rather than exhaustive, when we can truly see and hear all that Jesus taught not just with our physical eyes and ears, but also with the eyes and ears of our souls, we have to expand our concept of the poor and needy: "Kinship is the game-changer," Father Gregory Boyle tells gang members in Los Angeles. He offers work in Homeboy and Homegirl Industries as a route out of gang life. He writes in *Barking to the Choir*:

> Kinship . . . is the Pearl of Great Price. It is the treasure buried in the field. Let's sell everything to get it. Yet we think kinship is beyond our reach . . . Gospel Kinship always exposes the game, jostles the status quo in constant need of conversion, because the status quo is only interested in incessant judging, comparisons, measuring, scapegoat-

ing, and competition. And we, the Choir, are stuck in complacency.[30]

As a community of all the peoples of this Earth, we need to acknowledge everyone's value to God and to the whole community. We're a long way from doing that in the United States. So many families function as discrete units, unequipped for community, only for promoting our own selves and our own nuclear family. The ties that bind us to our extended families, people with common interests, neighbors, and countrymen in a democracy seem to be tenuous at best these days. We don't seem to care about how another is getting along or what his or her needs might be. We are in it for ourselves.

To be restored to the community and to the family, to the family of man, to the arms of God—that is the goal of human existence. For we all belong to God whether we know it or not. For human beings it is often a whole lot easier to take care of our own and reject the rest. To be hostile to those who are different from us, to those who worship another God or in another way, to those whose skin is a different color.

And religion, which should be teaching us how to get along with each other, often falls far short of this goal. Bishop Desmond Tutu again speaks the truth about our world:

> Religion, which should foster sisterhood and brotherhood, which should encourage tolerance, respect, compassion, peace, reconciliation, caring and sharing, has far too frequently—perversely—done the opposite. Religion has fueled alienation and conflict and has exacerbated intolerance and injustice and oppression. Some of the ghastliest

---

[30] Father Gregory Boyle, *Barking to the Choir* (New York: Simon & Schuster, 2017), 10.

atrocities have happened and are happening in the name of religion.[31]

When we look at Jesus, "God Incarnate" (Isaiah 9:6), to see how He behaved during His sojourn on earth, we see an inclusive man who was as at home with lepers and sinners, Pharisees and scribes, Samaritans and Romans—the whole depth and breadth of society in Israel at that time. He talked to women in public (unheard of in his day)! He healed, He affirmed, He called, He loved and challenged all He met. He gave what they needed. He did not reject anyone. It was as if the whole of the people who lived in Israel, non-Israelites as well, were Jesus's people. Everyone is a child of God. As Christians, as followers of Jesus, as we are all created in God's image; we need to live this truth.

Community is the nature of the kingdom of God where everyone is welcome once they have turned their whole focus on God.[32] Every person has the capacity to realize what is already true, but not lived: that we all exist in God at all times. We are already the community of all men and women and children. We are bound by the Indwelling Spirit of God; we were all created in His image; we all belong to God. Following Jesus means that we are in the process of realizing what is already true: that we all are His, but that as long as we live in this world, *of this world*, we will think of ourselves as separate, unconnected to God or other people.

I see that there is the whole community of the church, hopefully evolving into persons who can live in the kingdom where the fruit of the Spirit reigns, where everyone is equal and honored for their contributions in the service of God, where there is a true community. And there are the people who are not yet there who have the same aspirations and longings that we do, but maybe don't know it yet, who hopefully will encounter a follower of Jesus who will look at

---

31 Tutu, 51.
32 See my book *Thy Kingdom Come!*

them with love, no matter what they have done. And change their lives.

Chapter 9:

Restorative Justice

From the Parable of the Prodigal (or Lost) Son in Luke 15:11–32, we see how God treats sinners who repent, who come back to Him. One son had asked for his share of the inheritance and then proceeded to throw it away in shameful living. Finally, it dawned on Him that he could be a servant in his father's house—doing the same kind of work he'd been reduced to doing in the world, but while living at home again, so he headed back to the family home. His father was watching for his return and ran out to greet him. He brushed aside any confession of guilt or shame and celebrated his son's return, restoring him to his rightful place in the family. The father was full of love and forgiveness for his wayward son.

And with the second son, the loving son who had not strayed, the father also looked at him with love: "'My son,' the father said, 'you are always with me and everything I have is yours. But we had to celebrate and be glad, because this brother of yours was dead and is alive again; he was lost and is found.'" (Luke 15:31–2) Both sons had misunderstood the father: the one who was rebellious thought that his father would allow him only to be a servant in his house when he returned, and the second son was obedient, but missed out on all the blessings of the relationship with his father because he didn't feel loved.

As we take in the depth of this parable, we see the love and forgiveness that Jesus offers us. None of us is perfect, but still, when we repent and follow Him, God will shower us with love and forgiveness. God is waiting for us to return to Him, just as He waited for the people of Israel in the Old Testament to return to Him, to His laws.[33]

There is implanted in us the longing to go home, the longing to enjoy the fruits of a close relationship with God, to be loved as we are, just as God is longing for our return. Built into His creation of man is a restorative justice once we have seen the error of our ways and admitted what we have done and been. It is not that we will never sin again, but that when we have put God and the Spirit of His law ahead of everything else in our lives, we are forgiven any further times when we fall short. Both sons in the Parable of the Prodigal Son have to broaden their view of who God is.

The saying of Jesus's "to be perfect as your father in heaven is perfect" (Matthew 5:48) is not to be understood as advocating a letter-of-the-law approach to our relationship with God. The Greek word translated as "perfect" is *teleios*, which means perfect in the sense of wholeness and completeness.[34] It is how Jesus commanded our love for God to be: all of ourselves, all our heart, soul, mind, and body (Matthew 22:34-40, Mark 12:28-34, Luke 10:25-28).

As we repent, as we turn back to God, we belong to God. He, in many ways through His Spirit, takes us on a healing journey. He amplifies the effect of what we say and do. He prepares the ground in the hearts and souls of the people we meet so that they can see and hear better what we are saying and doing. All because of a principle of God's that we are welcomed back into the fold no matter what we have done, restored to being one of His children, once we turn back to Him.

---

33 http://www.shuvaglobal.com/media/israel-70-biblical-reasons/ cites 70 times the Bible talks about Israel returning to the Promised Land.
34 Strong's #5455, **1596**.

CALLED TO HELP THE POOR AND NEEDY

If this is where His love and forgiveness takes us, then we are called to do the same with our fellow men and women. We are called to offer them a place in the kingdom of God when they have repented, turned back to God. That means we let go of any judgment of them. We see that they have already been punished for what they have done. That they deserve forgiveness for what they have done and God's love through us. They are to be restored to their rightful place in the family of God. We are to welcome them, just as God has welcomed them. As we help them, we are actually serving Jesus. (Matthew 25:34–40)

We have many Biblical examples of God's restorative justice. Here are two: Moses, who murdered a man, becomes God's go-between with the Israelites; Saul of Tarsus, a Pharisee, who persecuted the early church, after an encounter with the living Christ as Paul, spread the word about the church throughout the Mediterranean area.

This is God's restorative justice, which offers love and forgiveness to those who have strayed. Such forgiveness is not a normal or even common thing for us humans to offer to those we judge to be delinquent; we tend instinctively to be more punitive and unforgiving. Even after a jail term, concrete proof that one has paid the price for their sin, we isolate the former prisoner. We may withhold benefits of citizenship, restricting their right to vote. We might make finding employment difficult. Renting an apartment with a felony on one's record may be all but impossible. In general, we ostracize ex-cons and continue to punish them even after their debt has been paid.

One example of restorative justice that rocked our more punitive concept of justice came in South Africa when apartheid, a government policy of racial segregation, was dismantled in the 1990s. The new Government of National Unity, through negotiations with the government that had enforced apartheid, instituted the Truth and Reconciliation Commission (TLC) as a way to heal some of the atrocities borne of decades of government-sanctioned segregation.

In the negotiations between the old government, which wanted total amnesty for its perpetrators of violence against the African peoples, and the new government, which wanted to honor the agony of its citizenry, a system of restorative justice was adopted. The perpetrators of violence could apply for amnesty, but they had to admit exactly what they had done before the commission. Victims could be heard in the court, sometimes while facing the perpetrator of the wrong done to them. Bishop Tutu described the importance of this policy of reconciliation:

> "Restorative justice whose chief purpose is not punitive but restorative, healing . . . holds as central the essential humanity of the perpetrator of even the most gruesome atrocity, never giving up on anyone, believing in the essential goodness of all as created in the image of God, and believing that even the worst of us still remains a child of God with the potential to become better, someone to be salvaged, to be rehabilitated, not to be ostracized but, ultimately, to be reintegrated into the community. Restorative justice believes that an offense has caused a breach, has disturbed the social equilibrium, which must be restored, and the breach healed, in a process through which the offender and the victim can be reconciled and peace restored."[35]

The TRC developed this list of five R's to guide the process:

1. facing reality
2. accepting responsibility
3. expressing repentance
4. knowing reconciliation (if possible with the victim)
5. making restitution[36]

---

35 Tutu, 42–43.
36 Mike Batley, "Restorative Justice in the South African Context," in *Beyond Retribution: Prospects for Restorative Justice in South Africa*, Monograph No. 111, ed. T. Maepa (Pretoria: Institute for Security Studies, 2005), 22, https://oldsite.issafrica.org/uploads/111CHAP2.PDF.

The purpose of the TRC was to restore a sense of community to South Africa through acknowledging the truth about what happened and seeking reconciliation and healing.

In this reconciliation process is an acknowledgment that beneath all the things we have done that are sinful or evil, still we are children of God. Think what it must have meant to be a white man who abused his fellow countrymen who now had to stand up publicly and admit his wrongdoing, his sin. To face the people he abused. He had to confess, to admit his wrong. I can only imagine that without that public confession, he might have gone on doing what he had always done. But with it, he had a chance to turn a corner, to repent and to seek another path in life. Isn't that just what the alcoholic in AA is doing when he admits his powerlessness over alcohol and seeks help from others to support his journey into a new life? The white man in South Africa and the alcoholic anywhere—sinners everywhere—have the same process. It starts with an admission of the absolute truth about who we are and what we have done. With that, we have a real chance to change our lives.

Think of Saul of Tarsus, a Pharisee and a Jew, who was harassing and punishing the followers of Jesus after His death. Then one day he had an encounter with Jesus on the road to Damascus. Jesus said to him, "Saul, Saul, why are you persecuting me?" (Acts 9:3–4) That one question turned his life around. He had to admit the truth to himself as he faced that question from Christ. He lost his sight in this encounter; so friends guided him to Damascus where Ananias was called by Jesus to restore his sight. From then on he became a follower of Jesus, preached the Gospel throughout the Mediterranean area, and helped to found the church.

When community is granted the highest value, love and forgiveness and accountability and membership in that community are expressed. Anyone who has done evil to another has not escaped punishment, even if they are never caught. They will live in fear, in defensiveness, expecting punishment anytime. They will always be looking over their shoulder for whatever evil is coming at them. There is no peace, no blessing, no grace in a life of evil. To violate our own innate conscience is to heap wrong on ourselves.

There is only one way out of the sin and evil we have done: to repent. That is, to own up to the truth about ourselves, and then to bring our whole selves to God with the intention of changing our lives and of serving the Lord. Then we live in the truth of the Parable of the Prodigal Son. There is such power in owning the truth about ourselves, even when the truth is shameful and guilt-ridden. It brings us peace and freedom from always having to protect, to defend, to insulate ourselves. We can live in the truth, in integrity. Trying to live peacefully while not owning up to the truth about who we are, about what we have said and done, is impossible.

Restorative justice is highly valued in both the Old and New Testaments. It reflects Jesus's teachings about serving Him when we serve others. It follows the ancient laws of the commandments in Levitcus, Numbers, and Deuteronomy. We need to ask ourselves if we, too, are following God's teachings in how we treat others, in how our country's laws are applied. It is not enough to just believe in Jesus if we will not follow His teachings.

These are important questions to ask ourselves, because the reputation of Christianity in the world depends on how we Christians live and act, and how fully we embrace all people who were made in the image of God, just like us.

Chapter 10:

If We Take This Call to Help Seriously

If we take this call to help the poor and needy seriously, as God's intention for each of us, what can we say about living in a fallen world? Aren't we participating in the sin if we do nothing about it? Do we assume that this great theme of the Bible doesn't apply to us? Is it too big a problem for us to tackle? What can we do?

It is our purpose to live in the kingdom of God here on earth and not to be beholden to how the world thinks, but—and it is a big BUT—what do we do with the poor, the ostracized, the lame, the hated, the oppressed? The Bible says twice (in Deuteronomy 15:11 and Matthew 26:11) that the poor will always be with us. It is not enough to believe in Jesus. We need to bring our thoughts and actions into conformity with His teachings. Jesus spent His time with the oppressed, the rejected, validating and valuing them just by His very presence. Then He healed them. He fed them. He criticized the powerful of His day. He taught them His ways. If we are followers of Jesus, what does He ask of us? The answer seems simple to me: He asks us to do the same. The difference is that when we put God first, just like Jesus did, above all we listen to Him in all that we say and do. Then we take on the specific purpose to which He calls us.

If we find it difficult to follow the "still, small voice" of the Indwelling Spirit of God, if we struggle with our calling, there is a simple strategy on display in Christ's actions. Jesus was always going off to pray; we can do the same. Pray, ask for His guidance, listen to His answer, and then do what He says. This is the recipe. It's simple: We're not of this world, so we don't listen to the world's solutions to problems here. We listen to the all-knowing, all-wise, Son of the Living God. We don't ask anyone else what we are to do. We go to the Source of all wisdom and do what He asks us to do.

And when we do what He asks of us, we know that He will support and guide and nurture us in this call. We trust that all our needs will be taken care of as we put ourselves totally in His hands. We know that we will grow in our capacity to serve as God heals and transforms us. We are willing to go beyond the world's understanding to see the other person not only as Christ sees him, but we see Jesus in the other, in all men and women and children. And this makes all the difference, because in serving the other, we are serving Him (Matthew 25:31–46, The Parable of the Sheep and the Goats).

There is a lesson, I think, for those who follow Christ, in what happened in Ferguson, Missouri on August 9, 2014. A policeman shot a young black man named Michael Brown, Jr., and let him lie dead in the street for hours. Immediately, young people were demonstrating in front of the police station, many of them not Christian. A number of clergy felt called to add their presence in hopes of keeping tensions from escalating, and keeping more young people from being hurt or killed. Black and white clergy people of many different denominations gathered between the police and the young people to pray. They didn't tell the youth what to do; they just offered their presence, day after day. In Leah Gunning Francis's book, *Ferguson & Faith: Sparking Leadership & Awakening Community*, there are many interviews with the clergy and the youth that detail how they got involved and what it was like. Dr. Francis, a dean at the Christian Theological Seminary in Indianapolis, Indiana, speaks of her experience and why she wrote a book about this conjunction of police and youthful demonstrators and clergy: "As a practical theologian, I took up the work of looking for God's tenets of love, justice, faithfulness, and hope, and I wanted to tell and reflect on some of that story using the experiences of a few clergy and young leaders."[37]

The next Sunday at three p.m., many clergy gathered to pray at the police station and again stood between the youth and the police.

> They symbolically laid down their collars on the altar of justice and made clear that their resistance was an action of their faith. . . . Not only did they voice their support of the protestors, but they put their bodies on the line and brought the gravitas of their moral authority to the moment and to the movement. They sent a clear message that they were bringing the resources and authority of their faith to the cause of racial justice.[38]

In their churches, they were praying for the people of Ferguson and the family of Michael Brown. "Prayer is a link to most expressions of faith," Francis writes, "but the question this prayer moment raises for us is: 'What happens after we pray? What do we actually do in response to that for which we have prayed?'"[39]

This where being a follower of Jesus comes in. Do we just leave it in God's hands what happens when there is injustice or neediness or poverty, and wait for Him to wave some magic wand to fix everything? Of course, we pray. And then we ask Jesus, "What do you want me to do in this situation?" And we listen for His answer and then do exactly what He suggests. For we are His representatives in this world. If we are to fulfill our created purpose, we must act where we are called to act; we must help those we are called to help. If we expect God to just wave his magic wand, we are way off base. We may not be *of the world*, but we surely live in the world! And we are called to follow Jesus and to do His will.

---

37 Leah Gunning Francis, *Ferguson & Faith: Sparking Leadership & Awakening Community*, (St. Louis, MO: Chalice Press, 2015), 5.
38 Francis, 9–10.
39 Francis, 18.

St. Teresa of Avila, a sixteenth-century Carmelite nun who affected the church tremendously, expressed this principle of serving Christ:

> Christ has no body but yours
> No hands, no feet on earth but yours,
> Yours are the eyes with which he looks with Compassion on this world,
> Yours are the feet with which he walks to do good,
> Yours are the hands with which he blesses all the world.
> Yours are the hands, yours are the feet,
> Yours are the eyes, you are his body.[40]

The Very Reverend Mike Kinman, dean of Christ Church Cathedral in St. Louis, describes the challenge: "I realized that this was a moment where we were being called to get out of the boat (like Peter when Jesus called him to walk on water, in Matthew 14:22–33) . . . That's the way we know it's Jesus. Jesus tells us to do something impossible. If it isn't someone challenging us to do something that we think is impossible, it's probably not Jesus."[41]

Here is what one of the young demonstrators, Brittany Ferrell, reported as her experience with the clergy in Ferguson: "Church came to us whether we realized it or not. I feel like church is omnipresent, like it's everywhere. You create church wherever you go if you embody that God likeness. It's not something that you drive to and you park and you get out and you sit there for two hours."[42] The clergy brought "church" with them; they brought the love of God and the Holy Spirit to support the young people. When the youth were arrested, the clergy helped by retrieving their cars so they wouldn't be impounded. In many other ways, they aided the protesters. But most

---

40 Rory McEntee & Adam Bucko, *The New Monasticism: An Interspiritual Manifesto for Contemplative Living* (Maryknoll, NY: Orbis Books, 2015), 16.
41 Francis, 46.
42 Francis, 63.

of all, they demonstrated to an mostly unchurched population that the church is real and true.

In Sunday school one day at my church we were beginning a study of Romans, and it struck me that God certainly does not think like we do. What human being would choose the chief persecutor of the followers of Jesus to convert and transform so that he could spread the word about Jesus throughout the Mediterranean world? Who would choose Moses, whom the Hebrews had mocked after he killed an Egyptian, to lead the Israelites out of slavery? I am ever cognizant of the differences between the way I think and the way God thinks.

There are a whole lot of arguments among Christians about whether being true to Jesus is a matter of faith or of works. I think we are addressing the wrong questions. The questions should be, "Am I following Jesus? Do I hear His 'still, small voice'? Has He revealed my purpose to me? Am I fulfilling it if He has?" Even before we can hear Him throughout our days in all aspects of our lives and work, we can just think about what Jesus did and emulate His actions. He befriended the poor and needy, the leper and the lame, the sick and bedeviled. He was present for them: they got to know Him; He got to know them. We bring our whole selves to our neighbor, just like we are to do with God, when we stand in the presence of Christ.

An issue in America today is the fear of becoming a socialist nation if we do too much for the poor. This fear ignores Jesus's and the Bible's call to help the poor and needy. Often the poor and needy are too preoccupied with day-to-day existence to look ahead to a better life. They cannot organize themselves out of the mess they are in because it takes too much energy just to survive until tomorrow. Their days are filled with this survival mode of living. Just a hand up—help with medical care, supplemental income, educational programs to show them how to lift their lives—can make a huge difference. In showing care in such ways, we are treating those who struggle under the weight of poverty like valuable human beings, made in the image of God.

As we step into our call, as we obey Christ's call, we learn to view the poor and needy through God's eyes. Listen to Mother Teresa of Calcutta: "We think sometimes that poverty is only being hungry, naked and homeless. The poverty of being unwanted, unloved and uncared for is the greatest poverty. We must start in our own homes to remedy this kind of poverty."[43] It is not enough to just feed and clothe and house the poor and needy, we need to actually care for them, too, love them, value them. Mother Teresa continued: "Let us not be satisfied with just giving money. Money is not enough, money can be got, but they need your hearts to love them. So spread your love everywhere you go." Love can bring us to people and places that are messy and probably dirty, and hopeless too. They're fraught with depression possibly, little hope, and entrapment. But then there is love. It is God's love that we bring, love that flows out of us to the other without us doing anything. Love that includes mercy and forgiveness, hope and value, and all the fruit of the Spirit: peace, joy, love, patience, kindness, goodness, faithfulness, gentleness, and self-control (Galatians 5:22–3), so that we can be helpful to others. The quality of love is gentle and kind and good. It is faithful and patient, no matter what it finds or what the life has been. It is peaceful and full of joy just in knowing another human being well. Someone who loves has no problem with self-control because he or she knows that they are loved by God and that all their needs are being taken care of so that they can serve the one(s) they are called to serve.

Listen to Jesus to find out who you are to serve, and how and what you are to do for them. Listening to Jesus is all the guidance we need. We no longer look to the world's solutions for the problems of the poor and needy; we have the best guidance there is with His

---

43 https://www.goodreads.com/quotes/
search?utf8=%E2%9C%93&q=mother+teresa+on+poverty&commit=Search

intimate knowledge of us and of the ones we are to serve. And those calls of Jesus to do the impossible? He will help us fulfill them!

God's invitations to us are everywhere, seeds He sows constantly in our lives, calling us to serve, if we will just pay attention to them.[44] We can't just fall back on what our church does, nor our friends, nor anyone. We are each responsible to answer God's call for us. And for each individual, the call will differ according to our talents and gifts and what we have learned from our own suffering. Some may be called to work in homeless shelters, but not just to prepare and serve food. They will be called to get to know the people they serve well. Some may be called to change the laws that entrap the poor. Some may be called to stand up for a poor person in court or before a social services representative. Some may be guardians. Some may adopt a child. And a thousand other things. The Lord has myriad ways for us to help others.

It is up to us to listen to exactly what He wants of us. And then to do it. This is the way we love and honor the primary place of God in our lives. And when we do answer His call, He will guide us every step of the way—what to do, when to do it, what to say, and so much more. And then we will know the pure joy of using all that is in us to help others. For when we are doing what we are called to do, we are totally fulfilled and full of joy.

---

44 Parable of the Sower in Matthew 13:1-23, Mark 4:1-20, Luke 8:4-15; Parable of the Mustard Seed in Matthew 13:1-23, Mark 4:30-32, Luke 13:18-19, Parable of the Growing Seek in Mark 4:26-29.

PATRICIA SAID ADAMS

Chapter 11:

New Initiatives

As I have researched for this book, I have been drawn to a number of different approaches to poverty that help the poor beyond the charity of our social services, both governmental and private. I've read about Mauricio Miller's the Alternative, about a school that has cut its expulsions in half in one year, about a program that takes drug offenders before they are booked and helps them with social services and housing; I visited a Friday night meal at QC [Queen City] Family Tree in Charlotte; I found wateredgardens.org on the internet—all examples of new ways of lifting the poor and needy, by engaging them, by looking to them for ideas they would like to try to lift themselves, new ways of restoring them to the community. So often the poor and needy don't need advice so much as help in gathering the knowledge and resources to do what they already would like to try.

As you read through these examples, just think of all that the Holy Spirit is showing us these days about the poor and needy. I am sure you have heard where else He is actively promoting fresh, new ways of securing help for the poor and needy.

The Alternative

Mauricio Miller is a social worker and a MacArthur Foundation grantee, the head of a social services agency who quit his job to start a program called the Alternative. Miller writes about how the program began:

It was December 1998, and I was at a personal low point. For twenty years the nonprofit social service agency I ran had provided job training and support to hundreds of young men and women, yet I was now seeing the children of my first trainees showing up and still needing the same services. It was increasingly clear to me that my work wasn't fundamentally changing things for the families I had been trying to help. . . . I also knew that my mother would never have utilized the services I offered. She would have considered them patronizing. To qualify for my programs people had to highlight their weaknesses, their deficiencies. The more helpless you presented yourself to be, the more eligible you were for services. My mother had hated that. She, like most of the families I grew up with, wanted to be recognized for their strengths, good deeds, and hard work. . . . A system to help that was primarily built to look for deficits was a fundamentally flawed approach and I knew it.[45]

Miller grew up poor; his mother raised two kids by herself and worked two jobs to do it. He recalls his mother often coming home talking about a dress she had seen in a shop window and how she would improve it. He believes she could have been a dress designer, or a seamstress at the very least, if she'd had the time and the resources.

Her story became the basis for the Alternative. Starting in Oakland, California, and firmly believing that building community was the best approach, Miller gathered groups of poor people. He gave each couple a computer so that they could track their spending, figuring that they needed good data on which to base their decisions. In the group each couple contributed a nominal amount every month to a kitty, which was matched by the program, and each month a different family could draw on that kitty. Miller would fire

---

[45] Mauricio Miller, *The Alternative: Most of what you believe about poverty is wrong* (Lulu Publishing Services, 2017), 5.

any social worker who told the clients what to do. He used their group discussions to inspire the participants' actions.

He tells the story of one group of five immigrant couples from El Salvador. For months, one couple had been mostly silent until one meeting when they announced they had bought a house. Everyone's jaws dropped! Most of the families had been sending their money home to El Salvador. Now inspired by the one couple's story, within eighteen months, every family had bought a house! Now, it turned out that the house the first couple had bought was not in good shape and the mortgage was too high, 65 percent of their income. Friends helped them fix the house up; they refinanced the mortgage based on the improvements, and now it was within 40 percent of their income.[46]

Another story in the book is of a Cambodian refugee, Ted Ngoy, who bought a doughnut shop in 1977. Fifteen years later, Cambodian immigrants owned over 60 percent of the doughnut shops in California. "He set a 'tangible example' of what is possible."[47]

Miller outlines three characteristics of the Alternative's approach:
1. Control: Let the families lead the change that they want to see happen.
2. Choices: Families deserve a range of choices like those people with more resources.
3. Community: Getting out of poverty takes more than an individual family effort.[48]

Miller's Family Independence Initiative was set up to demonstrate a bottom-up rather than top-down approach. "It shows that getting professional helpers out of the way leads to better outcomes."[49]

---

46 Miller, 138–141.
47 Miller, 115.
48 Miller, 128–9.
49 Miller, 129.

Watered Gardens

Another alternative approach to taking care of the homeless is the brainchild of Watered Gardens' James Whitford in Joplin, Missouri. He wanted to avoid a "para-church" ministry (like that of Campus Crusade for Christ), favoring a "church-servant" ministry.[50] Watered Gardens's values are:

> Relationship: Every person is meant to be with another.
> Redemption: Every person is meant to be with God.
> Hope: Every person should see an end to his poverty.
> Human Dignity: Every person is a noble creation.[51]

Note the inclusion of community in this list, as is emphasized by the Alternative. Watered Gardens connects one neighbor's need with another's skills. The homeless who stay in the shelter help out with the chores around the mission. Watered Gardens Forge Initiative is a 180-day training program in work readiness. Classes include Steps to Christian Maturity, Physical Wellness, Community Engagement, Healthy Living, Stewardship and Economics, Government and Legal Living, and GED prep. Watered Gardens is not just housing the homeless; they are changing lives, too.

Bammel Middle School

In Houston, Texas, Bammel Middle School was rife with students fighting in the halls between classes; teachers had a terrible time keeping control in the classrooms. Today, both students and teachers report being happy at the school. A report from the *Texas Tribune* explained how everything changed:

---

50 Watered Gardens Ministries, wateredgardens.org/about-us/mission-vision-and-history/.
51 Watered Gardens.

Principal La Quesha Grigby attributes the improvement [from ninety-four three-day suspensions to forty-seven in one year] to a simple schedule change at the beginning of this academic year: a carve-out of thirty-five minutes twice a week for teachers and students to circle up and talk about their feelings. Bammel Middle School is one of a growing number of Texas schools that have adopted "restorative justice," which encourages students and teachers to talk through their problems and build stronger relationships in order to prevent conflict and violence before it happens. "Sometimes those behaviors we see as discipline problems really are because the student is struggling with their academics," Grigsby said. "We're in a situation where we have to do something drastic . . . because what we've been doing is not working."[52]

Just speaking out loud about what's going on and being heard is a powerful deterrent to violence in this school—for both teachers and students. They get to know each other more deeply, and both students and teachers see something of how the other operates within the challenges of being at school.

QC Family Tree

Charlotte, North Carolina, (known as the Queen City) is home to QC Family Tree, part of a loose network of "new monasticism": community-oriented persons of faith across this country who want to work in inner-city neighborhoods for the benefit of their residents. Here's a statement of intent from *The New Monasticism: An Interspiritual Manifesto for Contemplative Living*: "It is an orientation

---

52 Aliyya Swaby, "Twice a week, these Texas students circle up and talk about their feelings. It's lowering suspensions and preventing violence," *Texas Tribune*, May 29, 2018, https://www.texastribune.org/2018/05/29/texas-schools-restorative-justice-violence-suspensions/.

in life, a commitment that asks us to bring every aspect of our lives into a living relationship with God."[53]

QC Family Tree is the brainchild of the Reverends Greg and Helms Jarrell. From an office in a poor, black neighborhood west of Uptown Charlotte, Greg and Helms run a number of programs for the community they live in. The phrase that best describes their work is "building a little village for the common good."[54] They focus on two initiatives in this neighborhood: affordable housing and helping children and families. They offer five apartments at low rent in their neighborhood and are active in advocating for affordable housing in Charlotte.

For families, they offer a number of programs. They serve dinner (with the help of local churches) two Friday nights a month throughout the year. They offer a pottery studio for the use of the residents. They were instrumental in adding another Freedom School in Charlotte (there are now fifteen in the city); this program provides summer classes for economically disadvantaged elementary and middle school students so they don't lose reading skills. The schools also provide two meals a day to the children. QC Family Tree sends sixty kids to the Freedom School they started. They also serve ten high school students who learn bike repair, take swimming lessons, work and get paid, and do fun stuff over the summer.

LEAD: Law Enforcement Assisted Diversion Program

This program in Seattle was started in 2011 by a district attorney who noted that punishing addicts wasn't working. LEAD provides support to people arrested for drug possession before they are booked. Instead of being sent to jail, those arrested are sent to social workers

---

[53] Rory McEntee, "A New Monasticism for Our Times," *The Catalyst* (blog), May 7, 2015, http://theshiftnetwork.com/blog/2015-05-07/new-monasticism-our-times.

[54] Reverend Greg Jarrell, in discussion with the author, June 25, 2018.

and receive housing assistance and other help so they can break their addictions. The program has been so successful that as of 2019, it is operational in thirty-eight other cities and counties across the country, with plans to launch in six more, and serious interest from dozens of others.[55]

Each of these stories shows us how we might help people deal with their needs using new techniques to solve age-old problems. The common denominator in these stories is the use of community to achieve results, to reform broken lives, to give voice to all that is bothering the students and the teachers. The bonds and ties among people are what help to elevate behavior and lives. As Bishop Tutu wrote: "The completely self-sufficient human being is subhuman."[56] It is when we are a part of something bigger than ourselves, valued and welcomed, that many of our problems get taken care of.

All these programs are supportive of the growth of the people they serve in many different ways, and all maintain the dignity and initiative of residents, students, and participants. This approach is very different from the top-down, more paralyzing approach of traditional social work, which is focused on the demeaning, more limiting structure of welfare.

Restorative programs honor the people they serve and their own dreams for their lives; they offer a whole new way of dealing with what we think are problems in our country. Each is suggestive of other inventive approaches that might manifest the vision and hopes and dreams of poor populations. Can you think of other approaches that might work to help lift the residents out of poverty? That don't judge the people they serve? That help restore them to full citizenship and participation in our country? That give them a hand to help them out of their predicaments?

---

55 Website for the LEAD National Support Bureau, https://www.leadbureau.org/.
56 Tutu, 22.

Chapter 12:
From Oblivion to Awareness

As I look back over the nineteen years since my husband died, I can see that I have been in training to write this book. In a way these pages mirror my own journey from being among the privileged white people walled off from the pain in the world around them to one who now truly sees the poor and needy for who they are, who loves those who are abused and forgotten, looked down upon and neglected. As a white person in a white-dominated culture, I assumed so many things, but the Lord began the process of disengaging me from that privilege soon after my husband died. And maybe He had already been working on me throughout my life as He has healed my own issues.

In the early 2000s I spent three weeks at the Mexican-American Cultural Center in San Antonio, Texas, working with people of Hispanic origin. I learned how differently some of them experience God and Mary and Jesus. Unlike the headier forms of Christianity practiced in the United States, theirs is a familial experience: Jesus is a member of their family, Mary their mother, God their father.

From San Antonio one day, we took a field trip to Metamores, Mexico. First, we visited a garbage dump where many families lived; they were gathering discarded metals to sell. Children and adults alike were barefooted there. We visited a charity that helped Central Americans and Mexicans regroup as they prepared to cross the Rio Grande into Texas. We met with three young cousins in their twenties who had traveled from El Salvador on the outside of freight trains all across Mexico. The oldest had been in the US before and had come back home to bring his two younger cousins. Soon they would cross illegally into the United States. Oh, what they had already endured, and what a horrific welcome they would receive in the States!

The year before that trip to San Antonio, I went on a ten-day tour of Haiti with a Disciples of Christ pastor from Oregon. During the week in the mornings we worked in an orphanage for sick children or in a hospice, both run by Mother Teresa's Missionaries of Charity. Since my husband had just died, I opted to work in the orphanage. There I saw ten babies per room with just one caretaker. Every other crib might have had a toy. I would hold the babies and just cry. What I thought a child needed for a good start in life—the toys, the experiences, a loving adult, someone speaking the language to them all day—would never happen for those kids. All the walls I had built inside me to keep out the pain of the world just crumbled.

During the afternoons we met with various people to hear what it was like in Haiti then—an American consulate officer, Haitian and other nationalities working for NGOs there.

During the one weekend we were in Haiti, two of us stayed with a village elder and his wife, along with an interpreter. Many teens in the village were attending a revival that weekend, held just outside the house. We attended, too, mostly not understanding the language; the interpreter told me later that I would have felt right at home, because it was all about hellfire-and-damnation—the kind of Christianity that I grew up in.

We were locked in their house at night, sleeping on the floor of the dining room with access to a chamber pot. The residents were afraid of voodoo worship, and particularly of a tree just outside the village that the voodoo people used. No one went out at night. One dinner, our hostess served us fried flour. The next day we walked up the mountain to the market. As we entered the market area, we saw a line of donkeys tied up along the way. Women, and a few men, sat surrounded by the things they were selling. We walked through this marketplace, greeting the merchants.

As I said, the walls in me came tumbling down during that first trip to Haiti. The next year I spent a month in Fermat, in the mountains above Port-au-Prince, living at an orphanage and assisting the physical therapy assistant with moving the limbs of the fifteen or so kids who were wheelchair-bound. Most had no language and seemingly little awareness. There was another group of children, too, who were orphaned and in school at the same place. For them I made up simple crossword puzzles in Creole.

This, too, was a great place of learning for me. First, I was awash in fear, and for each fear that arose in me, it would take me a day or two to decide to face it. First, I was afraid of being the sole white person in a sea of black faces. Then I was afraid of speaking the little bit of Creole that I had learned. And then I faced traveling by myself to Jacmel on the south coast. Each step was painful to anticipate, but when I took it, nothing happened. People were indifferent to the sole white person in their view. They expected me to speak their language. And going to Jacmel—why not?

The impression I left Fermat with was of the wheelchair kids who had no language: I am sure that they would have chosen to have been born again as they were! I was shocked, but that is the impression I got from them.

These experiences, along with interviewing for Crisis Assistance Ministry in Charlotte, have opened my heart to the plight of the poor, which is mostly systemically caused rather than the fault of the poor themselves, as many in our country assume. The last year or two I have been reading a number of books written about the experience of black Americans and others in disadvantaged communities, including Father Boyle's two books about his work employing gang members in order to transform their lives. I have learned about systemic racism. I have read Reverend William Barber's *The Third Reconstruction*, about a new movement to change this country's attitudes and actions toward the poor and needy. I have read *Black Theology of Liberation* by James H. Cone and Leah Gunning Francis's *Ferguson & Faith*, both of which offer amazing stories of church on the streets. Some others I recommend:

> Michael Eric Dyson, *Tears We Cannot Stop: A Sermon to White America*
> Samuel G. Freedman, *Upon This Rock: The Miracles of a Black Church*
> Pamela Grundy, *Color & Character: West Charlotte High and the American Struggle over Educational Equality*
> Philip Gulley, *If the Church Were Christian: Rediscovering the Values of Jesus*
> Toni Morrison, *Beloved* and *The Origin of Others*

There are more, of course, mostly about following Jesus, not as the church preaches, but actually listening to and following that "still, small voice" of God.

As I have taken in these books and what they say about my white life and the lives of people of color, I have had to acknowledge all the privilege I have assumed without question, without making sure it extended to everyone in our country. I have cried for the harm I have, though usually unintentionally, caused others. My eyes have been opened to see what is really going on. And all of this was led by the Indwelling Spirit of God.

Martin Luther King, Jr., stated this truth: "Strangely enough, I can never be what I ought to be until you are what you ought to be. You can never be what you ought to be until I am what I ought to be."[57] No one can be free until all are free. I don't think many of us realize or live to fulfill this truth.

---

57 James H. Cone, *A Black Theology of Liberation* (Maryknoll, NY: Orbis Books, 2010), xxi.

I think it's possible that some white Americans are afraid of black people because our country has treated them so poorly over centuries and continues to do so. People may project their collective guilt and shame and sin onto others and choose to see them as less than human or less worthy. The guilt of the white community has horrific roots: in ancestors who enslaved other human beings, who raped their slaves, who hung black people for their "crimes" in public spectacles, who sicced their dogs on black people with no provocation, who used water cannons to quell their rebellions, who killed four black girls in a church in Birmingham, Alabama. Some in this community continue their prejudice against a population that has only tried to find a good way to live in this country after slavery ended.

Native peoples and immigrants have received similar treatment, with great efforts taken to limit how far they can go in our society. European settlers built this country by confiscating the land of indigenous people and allotting a small portion of it back to them. Our leaders today call Hispanics rapists and thieves and drug lords to justify our treatment of them—detaining refugees in subhuman conditions and separating children from their families.

The sins of the past and present leave a legacy of guilt that fuels systemic prejudice in our nation against nonwhite Americans, trying its best to keep them downtrodden. Our system is punitive and unforgiving to those who need love and forgiveness most. As individuals who follow Jesus, it is our responsibility to do what our system cannot.

Chapter 13:
Conclusion: Trust in God

We cannot be free until all men and women are free. This is the truth of our creation. This is the reason for God's Ten Commandments and all the detail of the law in the Torah. We are commanded to take care of everyone else, whether they are in our tribe or a stranger to us. How we treat anyone reveals how at peace we are in ourselves. If we mistreat anyone, we are living an accursed existence. A community of all mankind is how we were created to be in the vast interdependent system that we call Planet Earth. We are dependent on every other person and animal and plant for our very existence. The more we ignore that truth, the less and less fulfillment we will have. We will be steeped in defensiveness, judgment, guilt, and shame for what we continue to do to people of other races and ethnicity who are not like us, to others who may in their poverty and need not be like us. If we want to live rewarding lives in which we realize our full potential as we were created to be, we will allow everyone else the same freedom that we have. That is the bottom line of all life: to not take more than one's fair share and to use that share to the fullness that we can.

James H. Cone, a theologian writing toward the end of the twentieth century, writes not only from a black point of view, but from God's own point of view of showering everyone with the same gifts. "Christianity is essentially a religion of liberation . . . any message that is not related to the liberation of the poor in a society is not Christ's message."⁵⁸ Indeed, Jesus started His ministry with these words from Isaiah:

> "The Spirit of the Lord is upon me,
> because He has anointed me to preach good news to the poor.
> He has sent me to proclaim release to the captives
> and recovering of sight to the blind,
> to set at liberty those who are oppressed,
> to proclaim the acceptable year of the Lord." (Luke 4:18–19)

There is no freedom in oppression for either the oppressed or the oppressor. There is no chance to enjoy freedom's fruits because what we do is so wrong that we are surrounded by paranoia and fear. That is the lesson of apartheid in South Africa and slavery in America and the ongoing oppression of black Americans here. Only freedom from fear and paranoia can free us all so that we can enjoy the contributions and energies of all the people in our midst. Then our society can thrive as we all can partake of our interdependence, the great gift of this planet.

The two major stories of the Bible, the Exodus of the Israelite slaves from Egypt to the Promised Land and Jesus's life, death, and resurrection, both show us the model for how we go from slavery to the world to the freedom that God calls us to, to live in His kingdom as we were each created to live. We face ourselves and our challenges in trusting our Lord and allowing God to lead us to freedom, to fulfillment. And we take along with us every other person no matter their tribe, their education, their skin color, or any differences. That is God's will. It is written throughout the Bible.

Here's Bishop Desmond Tutu again:

---

58 Cone, ix.

God is asking you here, "Please be my partners. Will you please be my collaborators? Will you please help me to change the ugliness of the world? Will you please help me to bring peace where there is war? Will you please help me to bring reconciliation where there is quarreling? Will you please help me to bring joy where there is sadness? Will you please help me to bring togetherness where there is separation? Will you please help me to collect and bring together those who are separated? Will you please help me to make my children know that they are my children, that we belong together, that we will survive only together, that we will be free only together, that we will be human only together?"

And so know, dear sisters and brothers, that our God is with you, our God is Emmanuel. Our God has entered the furnace with you. And our God is the God of the Exodus. Our God is the liberator God. Our God is leading you out of your bondage. Our God leads you into the Promised Land.[59]

It is up to us to align our will with God's and to bring in the kingdom of God here on Earth. Will you be one of those who will walk in Jesus's footsteps and be gracious and embracing to every person you meet?

In order to recognize and embrace Christ in every other person, we have to tear down the walls within us that allow us to judge, to be defensive, to be competitive, to put ourselves first, to only relate to our tribe or clan. All the egocentricity that is within us has to go. All the tribal stuff has to go. All the racial stuff has to go. So also the anxiety, the nervousness, the anger—all these have to go in favor of living in the arms of God. I don't mean to suggest that we do the healing work on ourselves. God has to do the work. We can't. Our part is to surrender all these sins to God; then He will heal us of these very human tendencies to favor "our own" people and ourselves.

---

59 Tutu, 77.

Then we will live in trust that He will take care of everyone. That He will value us and fulfill us and use us to our highest potential. That we will be fine no matter what happens to us.

This supreme trust—that we will be taken care of—is what allows us to embrace everyone else. We no longer have to worry about meeting our own needs. God will provide. We no longer have to judge other people, because that is God's job. We will know our purpose and be shown how to execute it. We will be accompanied wherever we go—no worries there. We will be fed and clothed, our thirst slaked. Every human need we have will be filled. We can live the wisdom of the Twenty-Third Psalm!

And so we relax. We have learned to trust God in everything. That is in EVERY THING! And we love and serve Him with all of ourselves. We love our neighbor as ourselves. And we fulfill our creation. All with God's help!

About the Author

Patricia Said Adams is a spiritual director, a supervisor of spiritual directors, a blogger about life lived in Christ, and the author of two other books, *Thy Kingdom Come!* and *Exodus: Our Story, Too!: From Slavery to the World to the Kingdom of God.* She writes through the lens of a spiritual director: *How do I, how do we, live this life we are called to?* While not a theologian, Adams feels that beliefs are only the entry point to a Christian life, that the life really begins when we begin to hear and obey God's "still, small voice" (1 Kings 19:12 KJV). If we follow the soft murmurings of the Indwelling Spirit of God into our own deeper selves, we will find our purpose and the fulfillment of our created nature in serving Him and others.

Adams is a widow with three grown children and their spouses and eight grandchildren, who are all the delight of her life. She lives in Matthews, North Carolina. You can read more at patsaidadams.com and deepeningyourfaith.com.

www.ingramcontent.com/pod-product-compliance
Lightning Source LLC
LaVergne TN
LVHW091603060526
838200LV00036B/982